This

or

Something

Better

This

or

Something

Better

A MEMOIR OF RESILIENCE

Elisa Stancil Levine

SHE WRITES PRESS

Published 2022

Printed in the United States of America

Print ISBN: 978-1-64742-361-2
E-ISBN: 978-1-64742-362-9
Library of Congress Control Number: 2021923160

For information, address:
She Writes Press
1569 Solano Ave #546
Berkeley, CA 94707

She Writes Press is a division of SparkPoint Studio, LLC. All company and/or product names may be trade names, logos, trademarks, and/or registered trademarks and are the property of their respective owners.

Names and identifying characteristics have been changed to protect the privacy of certain individuals.

This memoir is dedicated to
my husband, Chuck,
and my son, James,
whose acceptance, love, and humor illuminate my world.
And to all our family, both on the earth and departed,
thank you for the memories herein.

Contents

ONE: Firestorm, Sonoma Mountain, 2017 1

TWO: Where We Used to Go 9

THREE: Unearned Shame 16

FOUR: Even So, Present Day. 21

FIVE: Fear Not. 26

SIX: Proving Ground, Placerville. 32

SEVEN: The River. 42

EIGHT: Grandpa Again 50

NINE: How to Be Human 54

TEN: A Spirit Door. 59

ELEVEN: Unintended Consequences. 65

TWELVE: Subterranean 71

THIRTEEN: Trying to Make It Real 80

FOURTEEN: Wishing and Hoping. 87

FIFTEEN: Kenny Kenny Kenny, Seattle. 91

SIXTEEN: The Unknowable. 95

SEVENTEEN: Alchemy 102

EIGHTEEN: Out of the Echoing Emptiness 107

NINETEEN: Hallelujah Chorus. 112

TWENTY: Together Forever 117

TWENTY-ONE: Making it Work. 123

TWENTY-TWO: Rescue Me 131

TWENTY-THREE: Sacramento 139

TWENTY-FOUR: Pollyanna. 147

TWENTY-FIVE: Fragile Interconnections 152

TWENTY-SIX: Losing 159

TWENTY-SEVEN: This or Something Better 167

TWENTY-EIGHT: Sun and Shadow 173

TWENTY-NINE: Redemption, Sonoma 177

THIRTY: Kismet 182

THIRTY-ONE: Diamonds and Rust 188

THIRTY-TWO: Listening 193

THIRTY-THREE: Into It 199

THIRTY-FOUR: Coming Undone and Becoming 206

THIRTY-FIVE: Seeking Belonging 211

THIRTY-SIX: Roses All Around 218

THIRTY-SEVEN: Together 226

THIRTY-EIGHT: Just Plain True 231

THIRTY-NINE: Gather Round the Roses 237

FORTY: Glen Ellen, 2009–Present 241

Acknowledgments and Gratitude 246

About the Author 247

ONE

Firestorm, Sonoma Mountain, 2017

The scent of smoke, serious forest smoke, startles me from a deep sleep. My husband, Chuck, slumbers on. Both of us are jet-lagged from our flight from Prague the day before. I rise and stand naked before the floor-to-ceiling bedroom windows and see the familiar, dark outlines of the trees on our slope—no sign of fire. I go to the front patio for an unobstructed view, and there, across the valley, I see a blazing cauldron of flames. Fierce hot winds swirl my hair, and all around me the undeniable, insistent smoke builds.

I rush upstairs to Chuck's office and see the fire in the distance grow brighter, surging higher and higher with the wind. Our ranch, halfway up Sonoma Mountain, is bordered by forest—thousands of acres of wild land. Our redwood house is at the end of the one and only road down this side of the mountain. We are vulnerable.

I wake Chuck. He sits up, finds his glasses, and hastens up the spiral staircase to his office tower. The blaze is miles away, yet the smoke is dense—eerily dense for a fire so distant.

"It's not a little fire," Chuck says when he returns to the

bedroom. As he pulls on his jeans and sweatshirt, he continues. "I think you should make all the decisions. You've had experience with crises. I trust you."

For a second this surprises me. Not that he trusts me, but that he will abdicate control. For many years we dated bicoastally, and though we've lived together for ten years, we lead independent lives. But I see his point. Two type A personalities tussling for control in an emergency is counterproductive. Chuck's split-second decision makes sense. I will lead.

"Okay, then. Get your meds, your wallet, your hard drive. We're leaving," I say. My running clothes are beside the bed; in a flash I am dressed, trail shoes laced. I grab my laptop, passport, and wallet from my office and dash into the closet for my favorite jewelry, stuffing everything into a duffel bag.

Within minutes the inferno across the valley has tripled in size. As we hustle to the car, I grab two sheep markers from the junk drawer in the kitchen. Ranchers know how hard it is to identify loose horses in the aftermath of disaster, and these two giant crayons—one blue, one yellow—comprise my naïve emergency preparedness plan in its entirety.

Down by the barn, powerful winds push broken branches and swirls of leaves sideways across the moonlit pasture. Buzz, a black-and-white paint horse, and Brewster, a big-hoofed brown quarter horse, approach in the darkness and stand heads up, alert. We cannot get the horses out. Brewster refuses to trailer; he requires sedation, and we have no sedation. Besides, we lent our truck to a friend, so we have no means of transporting them. The horses will have to stay.

I try the markers, intending to write Chuck's cell number in broad yellow strokes on the side of the dark horse and in blue on Buzz. Though the markers have never been used, they are dried up and leave no mark at all. Chuck opens the gate between pastures, giving the horses room to roam, calling out to me, "Elisa, turn off the electric fence. If the fire gets close, they will break through and make a run for it."

Make a run for it? Fear courses through me, bright as lightning. How can we leave the horses? It makes sense that we can't take them with us, but now I see the bare truth. We are abandoning them.

"Let's go to the fire station and find out what's going on," I call back as I switch off the fence. The fire station is only a mile and a half away, in the small town of Glen Ellen. "We need more data before we can decide what to do." Seventy-mile-an-hour wind pushes hot air against the car door. I struggle to take my seat beside Chuck. The horses watch us drive away.

When I was eleven, a wildfire charred 96,000 acres in a California mountain canyon where my family had a house beside the American River. For days that fire raged, and each night bright ash rained down like falling stars. Standing side by side at a table set up near the road, I helped my efficient mother make sandwiches for hundreds of firemen and convicts working the fire line. The men moved past us, silent. Soot and ash, smoke and sweat permeated the air. My older brother was asked to volunteer as a sharp-shooter near the bulldozed firebreaks. To prevent the spread of fire, he shot burning animals as they dashed from the flames. The inferno raged on, and our family was forced to evacuate. That fire expired when it reached the river.

Now this fire, more than fifty years later, with its wild wind and eighty-five-degree midnight temperature—this fire is a beast. We are unprepared. As Chuck drives down the mountain, I retrieve a clipboard and pencil from my bag, planning to make a list to somehow structure the mounting unknown.

"Okay, listen, no matter how long this lasts," I tell him, "the only things we will need are . . . resilience and patience." I write these down. The rest of the page remains blank. I can think of nothing more to add. As we speed downhill, my favorite homes shine bright, each a compass point in my peripatetic past.

My husband grips the steering wheel tightly, peering straight ahead.

Resting my hand on his tense forearm, I take a few deep breaths for both of us. In stressful times I often make pronouncements, a way of coping.

"Remember, Chuck, everything we have, everything we have had, we will always have had. I mean, no matter what happens, the house behind us is everything I always wanted—and for decades thought I might *never* have." There, open rooms are layered with travel mementos. Family portraits capture a history of both want and ease, and furniture from junk stores mixes in with fine antiques. This is our home in the Sonoma wine country of Northern California.

Chuck remains silent as he drives us over the narrow bridge in the center of town and rounds the bend to the fire station. Before we reach there, I add, "Thank you, sweetheart." Gratitude, like a prayer, might serve as insulation to protect us from the fear, the flames, the unknown.

The station is shuttered, locked up tight. No one is there. All around us, big chunks of ash and ember fall and rise, trailing the wind. Next door, outside the neighborhood bar, a wild-eyed crowd stands clustered together in the dark. Cars begin to idle in the intersection, drivers in tears. Everyone is comparing notes on what to do. There is no consensus. The smoke is now so thick that Chuck begins to struggle for breath.

"Let's go to James and Cathy's house; the air should be better there," I suggest. They live ten miles down the valley.

My son James is away on business, but Cathy answers on the first ring. "Yes, come here now," she says, her French accent stronger than usual. "James is not home, but I am watching the news. Elisa, it is terrible."

Throughout the night we learn more about the four major fires in Napa and Sonoma counties. At five in the morning we read Facebook posts. Our entire town has burned. The mountain is on fire. By six, a neighbor's text warns that these reports are unreliable. From the top of the mountain, neighbors who refused to evacuate text us. Two fires threaten, one from the north and one from the west. Data is hard to come by because power is out, cell towers are down, and anyone behind the fire line is unreachable because they are fighting the flames.

At six thirty a friend texts from his home on an island in San Francisco Bay: "You must come here. We are prepared for you to stay as long as needed." The dawn, darkened by weighty smoke, brings no further data. The local news announces that Glen Ellen and towns north are under mandatory evacuation. Lines of cars slowly stream south on all major highways.

We hug Cathy and file out into the gray light. My short list on the clipboard is our lone compass point now. Sketchy reports of the expanding fires compound our anxiety. Despite our stoic vigil, our deep fear is plain. We remain within an arm's length of one another, eyes wide.

For two days, we text neighbors at the top of the mountain who stayed to protect their vineyards, their farms, their homes. They throw out hay for our horses, refill the water trough, and report back that our house remains unscathed. But we have to rescue the horses. Our friend Dominic brings sedation, and his rig and trailer and meets us outside of town. Mandatory evacuation means no access, no exceptions. At the police blockade a mile from our house, Dom idles his big truck forward and begins bantering with the police officer, inching slightly forward and veering incrementally toward the middle of the road. When our request for short-term access is denied, Dom rolls further forward, further across both lanes.

"Oh, gee, I see I'm blocking access with my rig; sorry about that. No room to turn around here." As he sweeps past the officer, he calls out, "We'll just go up to the corner and turn around." Then he keeps going.

On our road, we pass seven neighbors' homes that have burned down to finest ash. Smoke obscures all colors, rendering the remaining landscape in grisaille, various shades of gray. Huge oak trees are downed; trunks and giant limbs lie scorched in blackened meadows. At first, everything looks burned because even at high noon the heavy haze defeats all color. It is hard to distinguish what is burned black and what is just shadow. All is silent as we crest the hill.

That morning a neighbor retrieved our horses, and we find them safe in his vineyard above our property. While Brewster is being sedated, Chuck asks me to hike the quarter mile down to our house. "Just take a quick video of all the rooms in case we need it for insurance," he says over his shoulder as he opens the back of the horse trailer.

Trekking down the grassy hillside I feel wooden, disjointed, jerky. Two days of high alert have frayed me, and now, for the first time since this all began, I am alone. My hands tremble as I fiddle with my phone. There is almost no battery, and the signal is weak. Instead of videoing, I rush through the building, my heart pounding, and make a brief visual inventory. Even in that moment I realize nothing we have collected, nothing we have created is as important as returning to my husband's side. I race back up the hill just as he loads the last horse.

Eighty-nine structures fell to ruin in our little town. Throughout the county, one hundred and ten thousand acres burned. Shifting winds pushed the blaze over meadows and mountainsides more than once, burning deep into the forest floor. More than forty people perished. In the aftermath, burned cars are nothing but a puddle of metal, a testament to the intense heat. Only chimneys of houses remain. We are lucky. Our land, our animals, our home are unscathed. We still have what we had.

Three weeks later, when at last permitted to return, we stand on our patio gazing across the valley. For the duration of the fires the power was off, so the stench of decomposing shrimp, lamb, and beef emanates from the closed freezer and permeates the air. A blanket of ash covers the outdoor furniture. These are the only signs of disaster on our land. Across the valley familiar landmarks are obliterated. The grassy heart-shaped meadow on the distant mountainside is indecipherable. All is darkened.

Within days fresh winds spread vibrant autumn leaves over the devastation. On the hillsides, the charred earth showcases the glorious gold and red color. The seven families on our road who lost their homes say they are grateful for the covering. But recovering? This would take more than a course of seasons.

From time to time as I walk through our house now, more than two years later, the contents seem to lose color and density and to float for a split second in fizzy impermanence, reminding me that all I see is nothing more and nothing less than an agreement of electrons, a vibration, a collection of essence.

I became attuned to this shared energy of life, this essence, when I was about a year and a half old. My very first memory? I watched my brown shoes move over red dirt and sugar pine needles, and in that moment, I realized *I* moved my shoes along the path, under a big blue bowl of sky. With each step my joy increased. I raised my arms high and called out a greeting to the sun, to the treetops, to all I saw. But I had no words. I was too young for words. When the tree boughs waved and handfuls of

7

birds flew high, trusting the wind, I felt seen. That day my deep kinship with nature began. Some wonder how I could remember, being so young, but really, who would forget?

Since that day, nature has been my saving grace. This has been my story.

But now, looking back, I wonder if this bond with the natural world had an unintended consequence.

The night of the fire, when I realized we would have to abandon our horses, I felt deep grief. Yet moments later, as we sped toward the fire station, I failed to alert a single neighbor. As we drove past their houses I was busy with my clipboard, making my very short list.

Warning others of the fiery danger did not occur to me, not even for a second.

How could this be? What if someone had died?

TWO

Where We Used to Go, 1953

My early childhood was spent in the Sierra Nevada foothills of Northern California. There the dirt is so loaded with iron that it is not brown, it is red—nearly blood red. At a certain elevation a tenacious, low-growing shrub known as "mountain misery" spreads a web across any open space, covering the earth beneath tall sugar pines. At my grandmother's house, bossy new shoots of mountain misery invaded the garden, the chicken coop, and the wide gravel driveway beside the knobby spruce tree. The dull, feathery leaves of the dusty green plant exuded a sticky substance imbued with a medicinal scent. Every summer the mountain misery coated the cuffs of our play pants, our shoelaces, and our shoes with a pungent stickiness that was impossible to completely remove.

My grandmother, Laura, was a young widow with five children when the Seventh Day Adventist Church helped her move to an abandoned two-room schoolhouse in the rolling foothills of pear and apple orchards outside the very small town of Camino. My dad was eleven when his real father and oldest brother were washed away while fishing in San Francisco Bay.

Though one fishing creel was found on a rock not far from shore, they were gone, presumed drowned. The first year in Camino, Grandma and her children lived in a tent while the old schoolhouse was made habitable. My father and his older brother, at only twelve and thirteen, wired and plumbed the place, adding a laundry porch and an interior bathroom, and finished the attic. Grandma worked as a nurse, attended church faithfully, and applied strict rules to the raising of her children. These rules did not protect her youngest daughter, who died at five years old from a tragic fall. In the late 1940s, after Grandma's remaining children were grown and gone, she remarried. Her husband's name was Bill Bishop.

In the summers in the 1950s, my cousins, my brothers, and I stayed with Grandma and Grandpa Bishop for a few days every few weeks. Memories of this time are vivid, almost indelible. In the attic bedroom, we woke early to the ragged rumbling from diesel trucks warming their engines at the logging camp on the other side of the hill. When it was still pitch dark, Grandma would light her cooking fire in the woodstove downstairs. The black stovepipe ran straight up from the kitchen, through the attic floor, and out the ceiling. We could smell the chunky wood blocks catching, and, as the thin metal heated up, bright crackling sounds warned us not to get too close.

My cousin Debby was the only girl in her family between two brothers, like me. A year younger, Debby had palomino blond hair and creamy skin with a real beauty mark on one cheek, and not a single freckle. Beside the stovepipe we warmed our play clothes and helped one another dress. There was no bathroom in the attic. We used the chamber pot if we had to go in the night. When we were old enough, Debby and I brought the sloshing pot down the back stairs to Grandma's laundry porch. This was "girl" work, according to our older brothers.

"I didn't use it and I'm not carrying it down. I'm not even gonna look at it," Jiggs said. Oldest of us all, edgy and restless, my brother perpetually schemed, anxious to prove his power.

Downstairs in the laundry porch beside the kitchen, my grandmother's wringer washer and a double concrete sink spanned one wall. The gray concrete, whether damp or dry, emanated a perpetual scent of bleach and wet stone. The other rooms of Grandma's house smelled faintly of old walnuts and drying paint. Grandpa was always painting something. In their downstairs bathroom the short wooden stool we stood on to brush our teeth was heavily layered with a thick brown paint he reapplied every winter without fail.

My mother and father, aunts and uncles treated Bill with discernible disdain. An old drifter, he broke his leg and was treated at the county hospital in Placerville where Grandma, then about fifty-five, worked as a nurse. She read the Bible to him while he recovered, and from then on, he called her his angel. A strict Seventh Day Adventist, Grandma made Grandpa give up alcohol, coffee, and smoking. He never went with her to church on Saturdays, though.

Grandpa Bishop was included nominally in family gatherings. We never heard him raise his voice, and I don't recall him telling a single story from his past. On holidays at our house or at Debby's, he brought along one of a series of worn Western paperbacks by Louis L'Amour and sat off to the side, paging through it with his thick thumbs, his hearing aid turned off. If someone did try to talk to him, we first signaled him to turn up the volume. When I got a little older, I wondered if he actually knew how to read.

Those early morning summers in Camino, Grandpa sat at the long plank table in the kitchen. He spent most of his life working outside, and his short white whiskers shone bright against his weathered skin, like sugar on a donut. In the kitchen the morning sounds were quiet: the slumping of the woodblocks in the fire-box as they burned down; a small hiss as Grandma ladled batter onto the griddle. Her waist-long gray hair, unbraided in the early morning, shimmered as she swayed in an automatic rhythm, checking the fire, turning the sourdough pancakes, pouring the fake coffee she let Grandpa drink. Each pancake was the exact same size, stacked four high, the stack resting within half an inch of the rim of Grandpa's plate. Years later, when I began cooking, I realized it was not magic but her ladle that determined the size of her pancakes.

Our breakfast ritual was familiar, tender. Perched on Grand-pa's lap, I watched him spread the butter, then syrup, and at last cut into the perfect stack, a bite for me, a bite for him. He slipped his watch from the bib pocket of his overalls and placed the warm gold case in my hand, opening it to reveal the spidery black arrow, every tick a tiny, jumpy jerk.

"Well, Lisey, I've got to go," he would say as he closed the pocket watch, set me down, and took up his lunch pail. Most days he worked irrigating orchards nearby and returned in the early afternoon. Whistling tunelessly, humming from time to time, he watered the big garden, fed the chickens, and sharpened tools in his workshop out by the road.

Sometimes on Saturdays, after my grandmother left for church, Grandpa carried me to the woodshed, a kind of lean-to attached to the back of the kitchen where a giant drawer slid both ways (into the woodshed on one side, into the kitchen on the other). The rumpled stitches and brass buttons of his overalls pressed into my cheek, and I could feel the ticking of his watch, or maybe his heartbeat, as he carried me close.

When Grandpa shoved open the low door, morning sun slanted into the small shed. Loose blocks fresh from the sawmill were piled high, and I remember the sweat and stink of that raw, green wood. When Grandpa closed the door almost all the way, it was dark except for one thin line of sunlight where dust floated and curled in a sleepy golden swirl.

Humming a low tone, he lifted me up, away from him. Pressing my back to the wall, he pulled down my play pants and pressed his mouth to me, kissing me there. His rough, dry hands splayed out over my chest, and as he held me above him, I could see his balding, freckled head and wispy white hairs. I made no sound. When I closed my eyes, I felt like I was floating free in a deep, warm pool.

I felt comforted and known.

Afterward, I marched around collecting single blocks from the pile of stinky wood, adding these to the armloads he tossed into the big wood drawer. When Grandpa opened the woodshed door wide again, the bright sunlight flooded in, evaporating our private time.

Sometimes, when my cousins were napping or playing down by the irrigation ditch, Grandpa carried me down the driveway, past the scratchy, knobby pine to his workshop. His walk was slow and loopy, not brisk like my father's or careful like my mom's. With Grandpa I felt safe.

The workshop had three dusty tables cluttered with boxes and jars filled with oily bolts and screws. Whistling a tuneless pattern, he sat me on a stool beside the workbench. In the dusky half-light, he held my head gently with one big hand as he pressed to my cheek something velvety soft, dense, and smooth. I closed my eyes and drifted along, feeling warm and sleepy and quiet. Back then I was very young, much too young to talk.

On the way back to the house, I watched as we passed rows of sunflowers. They bowed and nodded their golden blooms in my direction. Raspberries ripened in a bright tangle near where the corn stood high. Grandpa picked a melon and cut some flowers for Grandma. On the back porch, he silently wiped my face and hands with a bleachy cloth from her washtub. I sat on the kitchen counter as Grandpa made four perfect loaves of the bread he baked each Saturday while Grandma was at church.

When I got bigger and began to talk, Grandpa turned away. We still made bread, I still had bites of his pancakes, but as soon as I learned to talk, he changed. Instead, he took my younger cousin Debby with him to get the wood, to find a bolt. I listened to his mumbly humming as he carried Debby away to where we used to go.

No mountain misery grows here on Sonoma Mountain, where I live with my husband, Chuck. Our dirt is dark umber, not red. Instead of sugar pines, our tall trees are giant sequoias. Thirty miles of trails wend through a forest of bay, oak, and redwoods. In the crease of steep hillsides, seasonal winter creeks sparkle bright against a tumble of dark gray stones, and in summer the sun warms the straw and bunch grass, sending a sweet scent all across the valley. These days, I run the mountain trails and sometimes hike to the summit through mesmerizing patches of sun and shade. These patterns, breaking through the canopy of leafy trees, bring to mind presence and absence, acceptance and denial.

Today I run slow and steady, smooth and light along the lateral trail that bisects the side of the mountain. The pace is painless, endorphins kick in, and all I feel is grateful—grateful to be able to run at my age on a benevolent mountain that did not burn in the wildfires, then return home to Chuck and all I ever wished I could have. The Grandpa interludes more than sixty years ago are ancient history. Too young then to feel repulsion or to register his actions as abuse, I experienced being close, then abandoned. Close then gone; sun and shade. Gain and loss. This is contrast. This is how we learn.

This is what I tell myself.

Childhood experiences leave impressions. Like fossils on a slab of limestone, memories are markings; they tell a tale, but only in outline. Looking back, I cannot re-experience the heat or the pressure that created the memory, yet the impression remains. Impressions add up and become a belief system.

Today I feel empathy for any child deeply imprinted by a grievous abuse of trust. By the age of three, I was already on the lookout for whom or what I could trust. Sunflowers and raspberries felt safe and reliable, and Debby too. But other people? Not so much.

THREE

Unearned Shame, 1953–1955

When we stayed with Grandma Bishop, we did as she said without question. There were consequences for disobeying; spankings, naps, and enemas. Consequences were predictable, but Grandma's moods were not.

Debby and I rode along in Grandma's truck to do "good works," errands like carting the smelly old neighbor woman to the store or rambling down a rutted farm road to gaze at a church lady's dahlias. This was the grandmother I admired. She was capable, generous with her time, and strong. But if Grandma began speeding toward home, spraying gravel against the bark of the knobby pine as she swung into the driveway, Debby and I stayed silent. A dark mood could follow. When Grandma began scouring the concrete washtubs and bleaching her cleaning rags, I knew she would soon call me in.

The lingering presence of bleach made my eyes burn as Grandma briskly stripped off my clothes, grabbed my upper arm, and swung me naked into the washtub next to the wringer washing machine. Blinking fast, squatting, and ducking beneath the scalding drips from the faucet, I stayed hunched and small.

Grandma scrubbed my bare skin hard all over with a short bristle brush loaded up with Fels-Naptha, a dingy yellow soap used for extra strong cleaning. Sometimes straight out, like a simple statement of fact, she would say, "You are a *murderer.*" Scrub, scrub, scrub.

Grandma's pale face would flush as she twisted me around, muttering the *murderer* word under her breath. The front of her housedress was soaked, and her fleshy arms beaded with soapy froth when at last she wrapped me in a scratchy towel and swung me out of the tub. I hastily gathered my clothes and ran to the attic to dress.

Anxious and humiliated, as I dressed I hummed a nonsense tune to backfill the dark questions in my mind. A murderer? What could she mean? I had no answer. How could I ask her? Who could I tell? It never occurred to me to tell anyone. She was my father's mother. In my world, she was God.

No other cousins or brothers were accused of murder. But enemas? Those could happen to any of us. A sturdy, line-dried flannel sheet would be laid flat on the kitchen table. Then one of us, naked from the waist down, would get warm water from the red rubber bag pumped up our butts. All the grandkids had to have enemas. "A good flushing out" was Grandma's cure-all for tiredness, crankiness, or stomachaches.

On her bedroom wall beside her tall dresser, a framed black-and-white photo of our grandmother's nursing school class stared straight out at us. Rows of young women in white uniforms, starched and prim, at the ready to fight germs. Church and nursing were Grandma's bedrock through the Depression, through the tragic accidental deaths of two of her husbands and two of her children. Did she blame me for her pain, for something I could not name? I only knew that scouring me seemed to soothe her.

At my parents' home in Placerville, about ten miles from Camino, my mother's sadness wafted through the rooms like a fog. My distracted mom was not compelling, only distant and vague. My exuberant and bossy father provided counterweight, but the dissonance between my parents created an invisible uncertainty.

At home one spring day I practiced counting, climbing up and down the three steps in our play room that led to a locked door. "One, two, three … one, two, *free* …" My third birthday was coming, and people smiled if I said "free" instead of three. On the other side of the door, a bit of lawn separated our house from the busy street. We were *never* to go out that door. This was one of my mother's most definite rules.

I skipped up and down the steps, concentrating, taking an extra jump whenever I said the word "free." My five-year-old brother, Jiggs, stood beside the door, hand on the doorknob, peering intently toward the kitchen.

"Come on, Lis, Mom says we can go outside for a walk," he wheedled. "Honest, she said. Look, the door isn't even locked."

Jiggs quietly swung open the playroom door, revealing the sunny day. Out we went. He took my hand as we dashed across the street and climbed the hillside, creeping low through the tall weeds. Loud creaking and screeching drew us up the hill, where we crouched to spy on workmen and a giant machine being used to repair the sidewalk. One broad, heavy chunk of concrete swung slowly, suspended from a crane. Just then a guy in a hard hat on the street looked up and saw us on the hill. He waved his arm hard, shooing us away.

"You kids," he bellowed. "Go on now, you get outta here! You could get hurt!"

All the workers turned their heads toward us. We had nowhere to hide. Right then the crane tilted, and the weighty slab slid sideways, slipped free, and slammed down with a *boom!* The man who warned us was crushed flat. As I turned to run, I saw an arm or leg sticking out from beneath the gray concrete. I was certain the man had been smashed dead.

We raced down the hill, across the street, and leapt into the playroom. Jiggs leaned against the closed door, breathing hard. He clenched my upper arm and whispered, "You better not tell! You'll get in big trouble for what you did."

What I did?

Turned inside out with terror, I felt the hair on my head shrink up. I heard sirens on the hill. But when I saw my mother quietly reading her book in the living room, I realized she never knew we were gone. Turning back to the playroom steps, climbing up and down, up and down, I counted, "One, two, three, one, two, free," until I was dizzy and numb, trying to get away, somewhere safe from that dead man. I buried my Grandpa's secrets and my grandmother's claim I was a killer. I told no one.

Two years later, riding alone in the back seat of Grandma's new 1955 Buick station wagon, I stood behind her as she pulsed the gas pedal on and off, on and off. She was convinced this saved gas. Grateful patients gave Grandma major presents: this brand-new car, a big television, an electric stove. I studied her, her cotton housedress and square shoulders, the little "x" wrinkles on her earlobes and along the back of her neck. Her long, thin silver braids circled the crown of her head like a halo. Lulled by the silence, her car surging forward and then coasting, I decided to risk it.

"Grandma, why do you call me a murderer? I'm only five. I'm just a little child."

With barely a beat of hesitation, looking at the road ahead, my stoic grandmother answered back. "Doesn't matter. Your mother is Catholic. You were baptized Catholic. Catholics murdered thousands of innocent people during the Crusades, so it's just like you did it yourself."

What she said made no sense. The Crusades? The only reference I had was a cartoon called *Crusader Rabbit*. I didn't press for more information. Her tone was definite, absolute. Out the side window I watched the rolling hills, acres and acres of orchards passing by, the center row always so straight, now here, now gone. I rested against the back of her wide front seat and let the mesmerizing pattern soothe me as row after row of pear trees opened and closed like a fan. We rode on without another word.

FOUR

Even So, Present Day

An email pops up on my computer screen. I sneak a peek, though I am supposed to be writing.

6:01 a.m.

hi, you rule! have a great day

My son, James, is up early. He often stays overnight at our design studio, the live/workspace we have in downtown San Francisco. The brick and concrete building is windowless, lit by large skylights and industrial lamps. The studio is a vault, the epitome of safety and freedom. When I leased the space I added a wide staircase and a bed/sitting room upstairs, framed by giant potted plants. Downstairs we have everything we need to be creative: vellum, gold leaf, oil and acrylic paints, gouache, every kind of brush in every possible size, and arcane tints and metallic powders. Here we develop samples for projects that range from 100- to 50,000-square feet.

We are decorative artists and colorists, devising and applying custom patterns for beams, ceilings, walls, or floors. Repetitive and generative, this work is a voodoo mash-up combining science, physical stamina, blind faith, and prayer. Creating transformation through color and texture is my craft; I am a maker.

Heightened observation, learned as a defense in my early years, helped shape my intuitive skills. I can read a space, a client, the light, the proportion of a room, seemingly through osmosis. My lifelong relationship with nature informs my palette.

Now, following thirty-five years of gilding, glazing, and patterning prestigious residences across the United States, in Paris, and in London, I began to crave space—inside a day, inside my mind, around my heart.

"We need to soften the presence of the architecture, create a space where you feel comforted, supported, and most of all *free*," became a familiar refrain at design meetings. When James was forty-two, he bought the business.

6:12 a.m.
   hi to you, J . . . inch by inch we make our way, right? we are the makers . . .

After sending my reply I scan a poem in a silver frame above my desk, a poem I have treasured for years.

Late Fragment

And did you get what
you wanted from this life even so?
I did.
And what did you want?
To call myself beloved, to feel myself
beloved on the earth.

~ Raymond Carver

Rereading Carver's poem, for the first time I realize he does not directly mention people. Did Carver also edit people out, like I did on the night of the fire?

My business relationships were short-term, conditional, transactional. Like Mighty Mouse, with my team I transformed rooms or whole buildings, then zoomed away. I've explained away bad habits—not remembering names, using a cavalier tone with my team (and expecting them to toughen up), forgetting or never bothering to learn relatives' birthdays—with one sentence: "I just don't care much about people." This handy dismissal has remained unexamined until now.

AFTER THE FIRE,
LATE AUTUMN, 2017

On our land, a long pathway cuts through the meadow and leads to a studio built fifty years ago. Giant oaks surround the 20'x40' structure. The ceiling, inlaid with a rustic herringbone pattern of variegated cedar, was installed as a tribute to the builder's wife, a renowned weaver and educator in the Bauhaus tradition. This one-room studio, designed for her looms and materials, was built of wood. She called it the Twill House. The floor, the planked walls, the beams, the countertops, the built-in bed frame, the bookcases, the deck on three sides—all are made of cedar, hemlock, or redwood. So much wood. Barn doors, one on each side of the open room, slide on a track to reveal verdant pasture on one side and a towering oak on the other.

The weaver died soon after the building was completed. For decades, the Twill House was rarely used. When we bought the land, we had the place commercially cleaned, top to bottom, and lived there for six months as we waited for our new house up the hill to be finished. Chuck and I traveled for work, each gone days or weeks at a time. On weekends, we carted our luggage in a wheelbarrow down the long path to the little house.

One rainy morning as we lounged in bed beneath the patterned ceiling, I stroked Chuck's cheek, turning him to face me. "I'm going to miss this time," I said. "Do you think we'll stay down here sometimes, just for fun?"

Across the room, a slice of high windows showcased lichen-covered branches of the massive oak outside. Glistening leaves fluttered, and I watched the mossy limbs nod slightly in the breeze. Chuck kissed my hand and laughed.

"Not me," he scoffed. He put on his robe and stuffed a couple of small logs into the firebox, turned the damper, and returned to our flannel-sheeted, electric-blanketed bed. A composting toilet, a double hot plate, and a wood stove that heated half the room made our stay somewhat comfortable.

Chuck installed a hot tub on the deck. There we stood, naked, dipping buckets into the water, dousing ourselves head to toe. We soaped up fast, rinsed again, finally jumping into the steamy water to warm ourselves through and through. We could parade around nude all day if we wanted; our few neighbors were many acres away.

When we moved up to the big house, we shared the Twill House with a series of actors, musicians, artists, a ranger, and a writer as a place of temporary sanctuary. From April to late October, the hideaway's charms outweighed the rustic drawbacks. Sometimes I use the peaceful space as my writing studio.

Finding safe ground is key after devastating loss. In 2017, two days after we returned from weeks of evacuation, I thought of the Twill House. We could offer shelter to someone who lost everything. Chuck agreed.

Through a community group we posted: *Rustic studio in a meadow, composting toilet, wood heat. Furnished. Rent-free to fire survivors.*

FIVE

Fear Not, 1954

Jiggs was six, I was four, and our little brother, Ed, was not yet walking when our family first started going to the river. Saturday mornings before dawn our father marched down the hall clapping his hands, calling out, "Hey, hey, hey! Rise and shine!" In the dark we all climbed into Dad's restored army jeep and took the steep road down the canyon to the South Fork of the American River.

At the small resort, the snack bar, shuffleboard courts, rafts, and diving board were empty in the early dawn. On the beach, morning shadows cooled the sand, and our campfire warmed us, crackling in a ring of rocks near the water. Mom fried bacon and eggs in a cast-iron pan, and as we finished eating, the summer sun crested the canyon wall. Ribbons of golden light reached down the mountain, parsing the high and low waves, making a mesmerizing mosaic of the slow current.

After breakfast, Dad stood tall and stretched, making a loud yawning sound. My father liked attention. Pacing back and forth along the shore, he flapped his arms; then with a yell, he dove straight into the cold river. When he surfaced, he always flicked his dark, wet hair to the side and grinned in our direction. Floating on his back with toes straight up, he looked toward Jiggs, then me, one eyebrow raised.

"Oh, Joe, no . . ." Mom would say, in her wavery voice.

Before long, my brother and I waded in. Hopping on tiptoe, we danced as the chilled water inched up our waists and across our ribs. The deeper we waded, the broader the cool river appeared. Our legs—white against the gray and gold sand—looked strange and bendy beneath the glassy surface.

Floating before us, Dad presented his long toes, and we grabbed on, kicking our legs in tight circles as he towed us along. The further we went, the warmer the water felt, and after a while we just dangled behind Dad as he backstroked us across to the shady side of the canyon. Perched on slick mossy rocks, we shivered and waved to our mother standing on the far shore, still and rigid, holding Ed in her arms. Before long Dad towed us back. We rolled ourselves in warm towels and settled sleepily in the sand beside the campfire. Mom sat upright beside us, silently reading her book.

Dad dismissed my mother's fears, scoffing at caution. "Come on, Joan, think about it. Why in the hell would they let go?"

But she had thought about it. If we did let go, my mother knew she could not save us. She never learned to trust the water; she was too rigid, too anxious. She did not know how to swim.

In my mother's small hometown of Orient, South Dakota, population three hundred, there was no swimming pool, no lake, no river, not even a pond. Her family's inner compass was set by life there. Irish Catholicism, alcoholism, and isolation gridded out their options like invisible longitude and latitude lines. Mom was number five of fourteen living children. Her mother, Grandma Rose, called these children her "stair steps to heaven."

Orient was a hot place in the summer, with one big tree. For the longest time, my mother believed this tree made the wind. "When I was little, I used to stand beside the tree and ask for a cool breeze," she told us with a mild laugh. Maybe back then she was like me, seeking signs and solace alone outdoors.

Mom skipped two grades and graduated from high school at fifteen. She left for Catholic nursing school one hundred miles away. When she got her RN degree, she enlisted in the army and served as a lieutenant in the Mediterranean during World War II.

The few stories she told me of the war were not about wounds or bombs or nursing. She recalled tea dances on the island of Corsica, a bike ride in Florence, a boyfriend in Egypt. "When the war ended, I moved to San Francisco and got a job at a wonderful hospital on the Peninsula. I never wanted to go back to South Dakota again."

In photographs of my family from the 1950s and 1960s, my mother is looking away or down. When I was young, I interpreted this as aloofness. Much later, I learned my mother was suffering from depression. Two framed pictures on my bookcase today show her before marriage, before children. In a close-up taken in Italy in 1945, Mom looks straight into the camera with a radiant smile. In Egypt, she stands in uniform beside her army tent, assured and glamorous. Back then she was in her power; the future was hers. After marriage, this radiance dimmed, and to us—or at least to me—my mother was more shadow than light.

My family visited Orient once. My mother's father, Fred Sweetland, was twenty years older than her mother, Grandma Rose. He was the town's newspaper editor when they first married; then postmaster, demoted to mailman, and finally just an alcoholic. When we went to visit he sat alone in the living room of their three-room retirement apartment, withered and glum. I don't think he knew who any of us were, not even my mother.

Grandma Rose was stodgy and pale, with wispy gray hair. She looked nothing like my trim, auburn-haired mother. On the porch outside their apartment, Grandma Rose wrapped her fluffy, loose arms around me in a soft hug. She leaned back to look into my eyes just for a moment, and then gazed past me to some distant horizon. Her pale blue eyes were set deep, like mine. Her steel-rimmed bifocals cast a square of reflected light on each cheek.

On that day, Grandma Rose roamed the place in slow motion, her short legs clad in medical compression stockings, her gait side to side as she moved about cleaning, baking, even ironing while we were there. A number of times she offered us lemonade or tea, homemade bread and butter. When she did sit down, she made a quiet sucking sound with her teeth, sighed, and smoothed her plain cotton housedress over her thick knees. Dad said Grandma Rose was "not a gusher." She was not even a talker. Her embroidery spoke for her. Intricate stitches decorated pink or blue baby quilts, squares of scenes from nursery rhymes, one blanket for each of her forty grandchildren. Grandma Rose never learned to swim either.

One summer day beside the American River, my father—thin as a crane back then—crouched beside me on a big, flat rock, his arms and knees akimbo. The cold edge of his big ear touched my cheek. He kept his hand steady on my shoulder as we watched the current passing by.

"Listen, hear that sound?" he asked.

I heard too many sounds: the surging rapids, wind in the trees, the call of a distant crow. "What sound?"

"You hear that sound like an engine running, that low sound?"

I listened some more. There was a rumbling underneath us, coming from beside us, behind us, sounding near but somehow far away. I'd never noticed it before. I nodded.

"Know what that is?" he said. "That's the sound of rocks tumbling in the rapids, underneath the water. Rolling under there for years. It echoes off the canyon walls. Look at these rocks. See how they're all round?"

He stood and pointed to the mounds of rocks on the bank, smooth rocks of every size and color lined the shore. I watched the shadow of his arm and followed where he pointed. Now I could easily hear the secret sound.

Dad stood tall, looking down at me. "How do you think that happens? Those rocks roll and roll in the current until they wear down, get small enough to roll away to another spot where they roll some more. You can't see them, but they're under there."

On that day, we connected when my father shared what he saw, what he knew. I peered into the frothy water and wondered, at six, what forces were invisibly shaping the world around me, maybe even shaping me like the river shaped the stones.

When I first started writing this memoir, I sent Dad some pages for Father's Day, portions where he was featured. I omitted any grim narrative. A few days later my phone rang.

"Daughter, this is one of the best days of my life. When I opened the door this afternoon, there by the door was your story."

Eighty-six then, Dad had trouble hearing on the phone even with his hearing aid. I responded, but he continued, talking over me.

"I sat down, started reading, read the whole thing straight through, didn't even watch *Wheel of Fortune*, tears streaming down. Listen to me; you got everything in there, you got it! Reading this, I remember things I haven't thought about in years."

He went on, sounding proud and somehow relieved. He told me to "get it all down."

This was the first time in a long time my father had praised me. I wondered if the first stage of Alzheimer's was making him kinder, more loving. I thanked him.

A few days later he called again.

"Listen, Daughter, you got a problem. Your basic problem, see, is this whole book. All this writing, this is about *you*. Nobody's going to buy this book the way it is now."

This time I spoke loudly. "It's just a first draft, Dad. I am not sure what it will become. I just have to get this down first, you know?"

"Well, listen, don't put anything in there about Bill, all that sex stuff, just leave that out."

I had told my father about the abuse when I was thirty-five. We hadn't spoken of it since. Before I could respond, my father hung up.

I put the phone down. On the hillside outside my office, the oaks tossed their craggy branches, waving to me, reminding me of Mom and how she used to ask her tree for a breeze.

This was June, the time of year I lose my wallet, misplace my phone, or otherwise break my connection to the everyday world. If I were a cartoon drawing, you would see phrases, unfinished thoughts floating around me like the dust surrounding that unkempt character in Peanuts. Murky half thoughts trail behind and beside me, a familiar nuisance.

June is the month my first baby died at birth. Midsummer? My lover died. Late summer marks the month my mother passed away after we finally made peace and learned to enjoy each other. Though all these things happened years and years ago, summer retains a tinge of grief.

For a few days, I let the writing rest. I find myself hungry all the time, wanting more and more. Finally, I accept that I am sad. I find my lost credit card and look up the exact date Mom died. I share with Chuck the sad irony of Dad's remarks, comments that echo my own fears. "Your dad is not your audience," Chuck says as he folds me into a hug.

SIX

Proving Ground, Placerville, 1958–1960

At my cousin Debby's house, everything ran like clock-work. Aunt Betty, my father's sister, managed her home with glowing assurance. And Aunt Betty was beautiful. When I was eight, nine, and ten, I studied her, intent on learning the secret of being a happy woman. Betty was the only happy woman I knew.

Was she really happy? Is anyone? Was I?

I decided to do an independent, scientific study and track my findings in a notebook. I gave it up in less than two weeks. There was no sure way to tell. Happiness, its genesis, and its trajectory, remained an enigma.

When I spent the night at Debby's, I invariably woke to the scent of Neutrogena soap. Debby always woke early and showered every morning. Betty shared beauty tips with her, and they used Nivea cream and Neutrogena morning and night. Their skin was lovely. I tugged on play clothes, then ran a comb through my medium brown hair, too short for a braid like Debby's and too wavy for a reliable style.

After breakfast, Debby slipped into the pantry and took two

packs of Fizzies, small wafers that turned plain water into a sparkling sugary drink. Closing the kitchen door without a sound, we crouched low beneath the picture window, hustled two blocks down the street, then ducked under a spray of leafy branches and disappeared from sight.

In the woodsy shadows, we transformed into secret agents. Debby carried our spyware, her collapsible aluminum cup. Opening it to full size, she filled it from the weak dribble flowing from a mossy culvert below the road. Dropping in the Fizzies, we watched as they sparkled and dissolved, then shared sips of the potent elixir. Fortified, we descended a half mile down the steep hillside in a sidestepping gait, past fence lines, barking dogs, and mounds of poison oak.

Digging into the red dirt, clinging to roots and low branches, we scrambled down to the back door of the Green Line Market, a cheap grocery store in the poor part of town.

We compared strategies in the back of the almost-empty store. With Debby on the lookout and my heart racing, I stole a pack of Domino cigarettes from a dusty carton way in the back.

Outside, in the speckled shade beside bins of decaying produce, I struck a punky flame on a bent matchbook Debby had taken from her dad's dresser. The stale smoke tasted acrid, but we braved a few puffs. Debby dropped the cigarette, snuffing it out with a turn of her heel. Without a word we stepped out of the shadows, prepared for our main mission—spying.

Our first target was the John Birch Society bookstore, a converted house adjacent to the market. Faded red and blue slogans were posted on the window, some a little cockeyed, making it hard to see any action inside. THIS IS A REPUBLIC, NOT A DEMOCRACY said one; and another, US OUT OF THE UN! Across the paved street, the steamy windows of the donut shop had slogans too, in the same style.

Dad said these Birchers were against *everything*. "Hell, if they spent as much time cleaning up lower Main Street as they do on conspiracy theories, this town would be a hell of a lot better off."

The businesses at this end of town were minor affairs: the strangely angled Chevron gas station, a messy tax office with a dirty front window, two real estate places (both closed most of the time), and one pawn shop. Looking for more spark, we moved on, hoping to get a glimpse of the man everyone in both our families called Hitler.

His walk alone made him stand out. With each step, he kicked his legs straight out, just a little. His terrier, pulling tight against a thin leash, matched this haughty stride. Our Placerville Hitler got his nickname from his mustache—black and waxy, painfully precise, a pinch against the old man's white skin. Debby and I liked to watch him for any deviation in his pattern, any telltale detail, some clue to his personality.

"What do you think he uses to make his mustache so black?" Dad asked one night at dinner.

"Maybe it's mascara," Mom said.

"It looks like shoe polish to me," I pitched in.

Why would anyone want to look like a Nazi, anyway? In Placerville in 1958, even the Birchers didn't go around looking like Hitler. Blue-collar workers or farmer types dressed for their work. Businessmen like my father and Debby's handsome dad, Ken, favored a slick, confident, Dean Martin style.

Over time, Hitler's waist thickened, his pasty face sagged, and his eyebrows and eyelashes took on a matching black rigor. During our spy trips, he remained unapproachable, a mystery. We never spoke to him, never learned if or where he worked, or even where he lived. For many years he walked lower Main Street, looking neither left nor right, accompanied by his dog. He may have been the loneliest person in town.

Childhood was a proving ground, a daily test of our ingenuity. Debby was Amelia Earhart to my Annie Oakley. Durability, likely inherited from our grandmother, was our most valuable shared characteristic. We were convinced we would grow up to *be* someone. At eight and nine, we were unclear on the details.

We could be anything, right?

When I was in my forties at a fancy dinner at Lutèce in Manhattan, Chuck's business associates asked me to describe my childhood in the gold country of Northern California. Before I began speaking, Chuck took my hand in his, smoothing my skin with even strokes. This was his sign for me to go easy. I can sometimes be too graphic, too revealing for conventional conversation. Before I realized the signal he was sending, I started in.

"Placerville in the 1950s and '60s? Just imagine a cross between *Deliverance* and *American Graffiti*." The stroking increased in pressure, and I realized, just in time, that this description could suffice. No need to bring up the benign neglect of my depressed mother, the scrubbing and fiddling of my grandparents, or the devotion to weaponry and animal cruelty of my older brother and boy cousins.

If I were to continue, I might talk about the Gold Rush, the perfectly stacked slate along the sunny side of the American River, a legacy from Chinese workers. Or about the creepy hanged man, a mannequin above the sidewalk on Main Street that dangles there to this day above the Hangman's Tree bar. But none of these things were necessary to mention at Lutèce, between courses, on a humid night in Manhattan with my businessman boyfriend. Better to conjure up a river, some banjo music, and a vanilla milkshake at a drive-in. Placerville had those things too.

The conversation shifted directions, and the evening drifted along. No harm, no foul.

When Chuck and I first started dating, he soon realized conventional situations made me antsy. I was fearful of being revealed as a rube, a fraud, uneducated. He knew I deflected this by being too revealing, too intense. His secret signal came in handy in the years that followed.

Up the hill next door to Debby, a small man well past middle age lived alone with his elderly mother. Wesley had a mustache too, but his was thin and gray, more moth-eaten than dramatic. His sparse, oily hair looked striped because white scalp showed between the marks of his comb. In the basement, Wesley taught piano lessons to children and worked on photography.

One day he called us over to his yard, asking, "Would you girls be able to water the garden while Mother and I are away for a few days? We can pay you."

Sure, why not?

On the first day, curious, we cupped our hands against the sliding glass door of the basement, but we could see only the side of the piano. For a few days we watered, then one day we arrived late, in the heat of the day. Leaves and blooms were visibly wilting. I braced a drooping hollyhock stalk while Debby got the hose going. The red clay was hard and cracked, and while Debby wetted it down, I suddenly felt a series of tremors in the stalk. I could feel the plant drinking!

"Debby, feel this, feel the plant drinking. People should know about this. Look how it's getting stronger now from the water. Feel this vibration."

I envisioned a future article in a science magazine, "How Plants Drink." But as soon as Debby moved the hose, I realized it was only the pressure of the water beating against the stalk that made it quiver. Dang.

The next afternoon, Wesley slid open the glass basement

door just as we arrived. The scent of Vitalis hair oil wafted our way as he stepped aside and beckoned us into the cool interior. "Come on in, girls—I have your money," he said, showing coins in the palm of his hand. Turning toward the rear of the room, he offered to show us how he "made pictures." We followed him to a small door. A light came on automatically when he opened it; everything was bathed in a low red glow. We followed him into the small room.

Wesley closed the door and turned to us, saying in a lilting tone, "All right, girls. Come on now, lift up your shirts and show me your nipples, or I will snip them off. *Snip! Snip!*" With his other hand he raised a shiny pair of silver manicure scissors, flipping them open and closed, open and closed.

Did Wesley take pictures? Did his camera capture not only our tiny bird chests, but also the tinge of shame left so long ago by Grandpa Bill? We don't know; we don't remember. When we left, we had coins in our hands. We still have nipples.

What Wesley did was more than wrong, but I had no words to explain his greatest offense. Wesley treated us like *girls*. His abuse uncovered more than our nipples. His sly manipulation revealed how naïve I was, and how vulnerable.

In all we did, Debby and I sought to rise up, to valiantly escape the weight stacked against us in Placerville, where we knew a *girl* was considered "just a girl." Already teachers were tracking us toward marriage and motherhood, as though it were inevitable. But in dodge ball I was too aggressive, in class too opinionated, in chorus too loud. Debby was subtle in her show of strength, but our shared strategy was simple. We each thought of ourselves as a *person*.

A person can do anything and be anything, right?

During those moments in the darkroom, I did not speak up; I did not push back. I was too shocked. And again, I told no one. What could my father do, immersed in his small-town success? My mother, distant and unreachable—how could I tell her? We buried the Wesley interlude. Debby and I had learned long before how to submerge our feelings.

When I was ten, I helped my mother set up the Republican Party headquarters in a small storefront on Placerville's Main Street. My play clothes—pink capris and a pink gingham blouse—were starched and ironed. Mom ironed everything, even the shoelaces of my Keds. I swept the open room and arranged bumper stickers and pamphlets on the window seat near the door. When I finished, I hopped up there and sat swinging my legs, waiting for Dad to take us to lunch.

A little bell rang when anyone entered, and the room soon filled with people. When the bell rang again, a stumpy old man shuffled in. His hair was so greasy it looked like steel. As he came near, I sat up stiffly, closed my knees tight together, and continued swinging my legs as though he wasn't there. His hands were puffy and chapped, stained dark in the creases, each fingernail outlined with dirt. He tapped his thick, grimy index finger on a brochure near me, then abruptly walked his filthy fingers across the leaflet, onto my thigh, up the front of my starched shirt, and straight to my left nipple and pinched it.

I jerked back fast and jumped down just as my mother yelled, "Elisa, get out of here!"

I wheeled away from the man and dashed through the crowd, out the door. I ran down the sidewalk of Main Street. After three blocks, I turned to see if Mom or Dad were following. Walking fast, I skittered further down the sidewalk, wondering where to go. The sun glinted off the chrome of slow-moving cars, and tears sprang to my eyes. Was I in trouble?

Mom and Dad picked me up down the street, and, instead of going out to lunch, we stopped for sandwiches and ate in the car on the way home. My parents were glum and said nothing. That night I overheard Mom say the name "Brunius" in her tight voice while she and Dad were having drinks after dinner. Later, when I told Aunt Betty an edited version of what happened, leaving out the pinching part, she asked, "Which Brunius was it, dear? Gary or his father?"

"I just know they said he was a Brunius, and he was old," I answered.

"Well, dear, that whole family is kind of strange," was all she said.

Even if someone had wanted to listen, there was no way to explain the alarm triggered by Brunius touching my nipple. This new violation was more disturbing than Wesley and his scissors.

How could this Brunius know exactly where my nipple was, under my starched shirt? How come it felt so electric when pinched, like a bright squiggly wire carrying current down through me? With this touch, the creep transmitted new data—alarming data about my own body.

And still there was the question of Brunius. Why would he *want* to touch a little girl's hidden nipple?

This question was like a Chinese puzzle box. I shook it; I turned it; I held it to the light looking for a clue. Finally, I just wrote BRUNIUS in big block letters on a piece of paper, then traced over it hard, in very dark pencil. I tore the paper into the tiniest bits and shoved the pile into the slot where my desk drawer slid in. Brunius, torn to pieces, was trapped there in the dark. He was dust.

One morning soon after, I woke up feeling inexplicably lucky. Lucky as gold. Small squares of light shimmered beside my pillow and across the corner of the ceiling, reflections from my water glass next to the bed. The air moved just a fraction too, like someone had just walked by. I looked around expecting a clue, some secret message left behind. I tried to think of a word for my lucky golden feeling—the air, the light. I got my pencil and sat at my desk. On a clean piece of paper, I wrote in pretty letters: *S u c h n e s s.*

Written down, it seemed good, but out loud "suchness" sounded weird. A little too much? Maybe I *was* too much, like my mother said. I was a Brownie, then a Girl Scout. I wrote poems and stories, won poster and essay contests. Mom didn't like me tearing around the beach like a tomboy, lifting weights with my older brother, making up weird experiments, and painting my bedroom furniture with house paint from the storage room. She wanted me to sit still and read, like her. I did read stacks and stacks of books, but nothing calmed me more than being outside, running free.

I vowed then I would rather be too much, call myself lucky, and learn how to guard it, than be like a Wesley or Brunius, a dried-up leech stealing the light from little girls. I like to imagine suchness, or essence, runs like a golden thread through all of my days, sometimes gleaming bright, other times subterranean.

That alarming fiddling by Wesley and Brunius made me feel powerless and blind. Focusing on the *wrongness* gave me no solace. Clarity finally came when morning sunlight illuminated my bedroom and patterns danced across the ceiling. I felt imbued with a private golden grace. Suchness, the shared border between opposites, is the sweet spot between freedom and safety. Suchness is what everyone craves.

In the early '90s, Chuck taught a class at Rutgers about entrepreneurship. He suggested I write a purpose and vision statement, a deeper, more personal version of a mission statement. My first attempt was a dry recitation with no juice. Chuck pointed out that my clients were interested in me as an artist. It would be best to focus on that. "Just be yourself," he suggested, "and see what happens."

The second round:

I do this work to keep open a channel for prayer. I create colors and patterns to bring balance and energy to my clients. I am sustained by their happiness as they clap their hands in joy. We prosper. Thank you, God.

On the same piece of paper, I listed, in the present tense, my five-year plan:

Penetrate the California market
Get published in Architectural Digest
Work on both coasts
Travel to Europe for research

Within a year my work was featured on the cover of *Architectural Digest*. Within three years my finishes appeared in *Elle Décor*, *House and Garden*, and *House Beautiful* as well as *Vogue*, *Town and Country*, and *Elle*. In the design world, my natural kinetic energy and intuitive, self-taught style were valued. Now I was not "too much."

SEVEN

The River

When I return to the South Fork of the American River all these years later, nothing seems changed. One mile past our house, I hike downriver, and here the familiar, eerie quiet persists. The river runs deep and slow, silent patterns simmer up, and then, without warning, melt away.

During the California Gold Rush, a century and a half ago, Chinese workers dynamited huge chunks of vertical shale here on the sunny side of the canyon and stacked slate high, flat, and tight for seven long miles, leveling the dips between hogback hills. What remains today? The well-built trail, three abandoned ore carts, and whatever the trees, rocks, and water recall.

The absence of change, the pure aloneness is reassuring.

In a crease between hills, I search for the seasonal waterfall where, beneath the cascading ferns each spring, I built fairy houses, embedding tiny stepping-stones in the dewy moss. The miniature half-timber buildings I pressed into the creek bank had chunks of bark for doors and big wet leaves for roofs. I was fourteen the last time I checked for fairies beside this creek. Now, fifty years later no water flows over the tumble of dry rocks and crisp dead moss.

I find no sign of fairies. It's too hot. Too dry.

Like a giant heartbeat, the August sun pumps heavy heat onto every rock and limb on this side of the canyon. Stepping carefully, pounding the ground three times with a thick stick, I call out my childhood chant: "Snakes, don't scare me, and I won't scare you." The sound evaporates, answered by no call from a bird, no rustle from a lizard. If I were a stranger here, this might be unsettling. But then a minor riffle, a faint breeze spreads over me, a subtle confirmation. I feel seen. I am known. I belong.

I turn back upriver toward the frothy rapids and sunny beach where Dad built our house in 1961, when I was eleven. Clumps of scotch broom and redbud still dot the wide shore below the low, mid-century modern house. Across the river, on the steep, shady north side, long Tarzan vines still hang from tall trees all the way down to the ground.

As the sun fades, dropping behind the canyon rim, I head upriver toward my car. Gliding swallows sail past me, their wings cutting the warm air. Their mud nests cluster in the high trestles of the bridge, the bridge where I used to hide and ponder what would, what could, become of me.

I recall my father's friends laughing, smirking over their scotch and sodas and whiskey sours at one of my parents' cocktail parties, while Dad, arms waving, described the dream home he planned to build. I overheard a man quietly ask the guy next to him, "Geez. Why would anyone want to live down in that hellhole?"

Back then, six haphazard tarpaper shacks dotted the flats near the bridge, and one old house, sheltered beneath a canopy of trees, stood beside an avalanche of slate slag more than two hundred feet high. Spooky? Not to me. All around, the murmur of the rapids echoed in the air with reassuring sameness. The trees, the breeze, and the patterns in the current were chapter and verse of an illuminated manuscript, offering up an encyclopedia of essence.

Dad's businesses prospered, and our expansive, modern house, twice the size of any house we'd had before, was soon underway. Mom reluctantly went along with Dad's dream, but her lack of enthusiasm caused friction between them. He could afford decorators and fancy materials and no doubt expected appreciation for his generosity.

"What in the hell is your problem?" he asked more than once in their late-night arguments. Deciding on wallpaper, paint, marble, and carpet was excruciating for my mother. It was a little like asking her to decorate her own coffin. Placerville was already the hinterlands, and now she would live in the absolute hinterland of the hinterlands. Furniture shopping left her in tears, and I overheard her lament to a decorator, "I know blue and green are *the* modern combination, but when I was a girl, they said blue and green should never be seen."

As her anxiety increased, the tenaciousness that propelled her from Orient, South Dakota, and later through the long war perhaps gave her the determination to see the building project through. But by late in that long year her disenchantment spread like a virus, and I avoided her lest I catch it.

Construction took longer than planned, and when our tract house in town was sold, our family moved temporarily to the ramshackle house by the bridge. Jiggs was thirteen, I was eleven, and Ed was eight. Out the back door of the one-bedroom house was a rough, dark shed where my brothers' bedroom was set up.

Television reception in the canyon was abysmal. Squirrels chewed through the wire running two miles down the mountain to our house. Dad said it would cost a lot to put the wire underground. "How would you kids like to have no TV? We could go on a big summer vacation every year instead."

We gave up TV.

We had the river, chess, reading, and music. These diversions were plenty for Ed and me. But Jiggs was not into chess, he didn't play piano, and he missed his shows. Cut off from *The Adventures of Jim Bowie*, *Sky King*, and *Davy Crockett*, he turned to *Guns and Ammo* magazine and a series of books titled *Chesty Puller, Marine*. He spent hours cleaning his guns—deer rifles, antique Bisley revolvers, a .22 caliber rifle, and a shotgun. He bought a shell re-loader, and I heard the whooshing, pounding sound repeating over and over like a slow old washing machine as shells stacked up in neat boxes. He was ready, but for what?

"Listen, when the Commies come running over the hill on the north side of the river, I'm gonna sit here and pick 'em off," he explained as he oiled the gleaming barrel of his rifle. He bought a crossbow and some skinning knives and started hunting game, wearing camouflage and smudging black under his eyes, using foul-smelling coon lure to mask whatever man scent he had at thirteen. He named his German shorthair hunting dog Shot.

I was the lucky one. My sun porch bedroom was just big enough for my twin bed and desk. The French windows on two sides and a French door looked out to the world. Here the air was fresh and light. Summer mornings I coasted my bike a half-mile to my friend Linda's place; her parents owned the cabins and beach resort where my family spent so many summers. Linda was slighter than me, with hundreds of freckles and ginger hair. When we went swimming, her thick, super dark, spiky eyelashes made her eyes look like stars.

For hours we explored the quiet backwater above the main swimming hole, drifting on inner tubes in the sheltering shade of shore willows, drowsing in lazy circles draped over our tubes until the undersides of our arms were rashy from the rubber. We tracked skipper bugs and minnows, built temporary dams to trap the miniscule transparent fish, and then, one hand scooping through the cool sand, graciously set them free. Sheltered beneath the canopy of branches, we hardly spoke. Kinship with nature was our common bond.

The first Christmas at the river, our new house still wasn't ready. We were roughing it in the old house by the bridge. Cold rain leaked into my brothers' cabin, and in the main house, the Franklin fireplace heated only half the pine-paneled living room. My parents argued or said nothing whenever they were together. More than one afternoon, I saw my mother leaning against the kitchen sink, looking out the window toward the bridge, tears streaming down her face.

As dusk darkened the canyon on Christmas Eve, Dad hauled an armload of logs into the living room and dropped them loudly onto the slate hearth.

"Elisa, get away from that window. You're bumping the Christmas tree," he barked. "The German and his kid are not going to get here any faster with you breathing on the glass. Go help your mother in the kitchen." Dad called his new accountant, Karl Dietrich, "the German." Sometimes, when only our family was around, Dad called him "the Nazi." When Mom gave a loud sigh Dad would snap, "Well, he's from Germany, and he lost a leg in the war, so you figure it out."

Our traditional Christmas tree, a silvertip fir, looked weird. Rigid, perfectly spaced branches held strands of tinsel Dad insisted we apply one strand at a time, pulling each into place, long and even, so that each ornament was nestled behind its own symmetrical silver curtain. In this rambling old house, the tree looked overly bright and prissy. I felt pinched and overly bright too, waiting to meet this boy and his father who had only one leg. They were late. Tommy's parents were getting a divorce, and he lived with his mother in San Francisco. Mom said he would be in Placerville for holidays and every summer. We didn't know any kids who lived in two places. We didn't even know anyone whose parents were divorced. Tommy was the same age as Jiggs, and Mom said we should make him feel welcome.

When our guests arrived, I saw right away that Tommy's dad was nothing like my handsome father. Karl was balding, short, with a broad chest and a soft, amenable expression. With his tweed sport coat and quiet ways, he blended into the background. I checked for a limp but didn't see anything. Tommy looked like a teenage Steve McQueen and, though not exactly shy, was reserved, maybe sad.

Jiggs had killed and dressed a pheasant and seven quail for our dinner. Mom made a rustic Christmas meal with wild rice instead of stuffing. The pheasant and quail had a lot of birdshot scattered through, so we each picked around this, focusing on the wild rice and salad more than the bony birds. After dinner, when Dad and Karl sat down to play chess, I noticed Karl's right leg was kind of stiff. That was probably the artificial one. By the time we kids finished our two-hour Monopoly game, I was deep into my very first crush. Tommy.

Tommy came to the river almost every day of my twelfth summer. When we swam the rapids, he looked out for me. When exploring a new dive spot, he let me go first sometimes. If we were all straggling up the hot slate trail, he would look back to see if I was coming along all right. I could tell I was still a little kid to him, but all through the summer, I rotated around him like the moon around the sun, hoping to catch his light.

Early the following school year, Tommy's mother hung herself. Just the summer before, Linda's aunt used a shotgun in one of the cabins at the resort, ruining the interior with a bloody blast. Could the ever-present sadness in my own mother pull her down, deep down and away?

Was she sad enough to take her own life? I couldn't imagine finding my mother swinging from a rope in our garage. When I pondered the mystery of despair, my questions seemed unanswerable.

I practiced lifesaving at the city pool, and in Girl Scouts we trained for emergencies. Before my family moved to the river, we lived near a dangerous curve on a narrow road, and sometimes we'd hear a heavy crash. "Elisa, bring the rags," Mom would call out as she sprinted to the wreck. She stanched bleeding and reassured the injured. Her nursing skill was impressive, always calm and sure. My job was to stand by and hand her whatever she needed. When we moved to the river, she brought the rags and kept them in a kitchen drawer like before.

But Tommy's loss was not this kind of emergency. His mother's death was a silent, bloodless wound. Now Tommy would live in Placerville full time.

"Mom, I have to bake Tommy a chocolate cake, with frosting. Can you take me to Karl's so I can leave the cake before they get home?"

Mom gave me (and my uneven chocolate layer cake) a ride up the canyon. She left me on my own for an hour to do my work. I'd been inside the modern glass-and-wood place once before and had glanced into Karl's bedroom from the hallway, half-dreading the creepy thrill of spotting an extra artificial leg. I didn't see a prosthetic then, and this time I was not there to spy. I dusted and swept. I found a tablecloth for the bare table, and in the center, I placed the cake.

They came by our new house on the river a few days later. Karl sat talking with my mother in low tones in the kitchen while we kids went down to the shore. The canyon was bitter cold. After a heavy rain, the current ran extra high, glassy smooth, dark as obsidian. Jiggs and Tommy hurled rocks and sticks into the sleek water while Ed ran in circles, throwing long willow spears into the sand bank. I stood back. Tommy faced the rushing water, never looking my way. It turned colder. Shivering, I hiked up to the house. When I opened the door, both Mom and Karl looked up, startled. Later I would learn why.

Tommy never said a word about the cake or the few wildflowers I left on the table or about his mother. Like me, he had chosen the code of silence, like a shield.

EIGHT

Grandpa Again, 1962

At the end of that summer, when I was twelve and Debby was eleven, we went to Camino to help Grandma box up donations of clothes and books. While we were working, Grandma came into the living room holding a small hardbound book in one hand. "You girls might like to read this journal I wrote when I took a train across the country. This was years ago; I was just a little older than you both are now."

She handed me the small diary and returned to the kitchen. Leafing quickly through it, I saw that her cramped, neat writing filled every page. I flushed in irritation, repelled. I didn't want to know my grandmother's young girl dreams. Why should I when she had tried to scrub me senseless so many years ago? I handed the book across to Debby without a word. Debby glanced at it briefly, then passed it back. I surreptitiously inserted the journal between Grandma's Bible and her nursing texts on the bookshelf nearby, pushing it in deep—out of sight, out of mind.

That same afternoon, Grandma announced she was going to Florida with a friend from church. Grandpa would stay home to take care of the garden, the chickens, and the cat. Without thinking, I nudged Debby, my compatriot in adventure.

"Hey, Deb, let's make a dinner for Grandpa when Grandma is away. We can make fried chicken and mashed potatoes and gravy." We'd watched Grandma fry chicken. How hard could it be? Some chicken, a pan, a spatula.

"Well, okay," Debby said in her even, agreeable way. "We could come up on Saturday morning, I guess."

A decade had passed since we were toddlers, since Grandpa took us with him to the woodshed and his workshop by the road. I never thought of those days. Neither Debby nor I had spoken of those times, not once.

We arrived with some chicken and potatoes and our overnight bags, ready to make a bona fide fancy dinner. About halfway through, I realized we were in over our heads. Our disappointing chicken was raw, even a little bloody on the inside, and already getting burned on the outside. And gravy? Mine was a lumpy, watery mess with too much salt and pepper. I kept adding flour, anxious to have at least one thing turn out right, and while we were mashing the potatoes, the gravy turned gelatinous.

"That ladle stood straight up in the gravy boat," Grandpa would later tell everyone. He was the only one to ever mention the dinner, or that night. Debby and I never said a word, not even to each other. Not for decades.

After clearing the greasy mess of a meal, Debby and I headed to the attic to change into our pajamas. Grandpa called us down, saying, "Girls, it's too cold to sleep up there tonight, Laurie said you girls should sleep with me, in our bed."

Maybe she would say that. Things were different at Grandma's house. Winter mornings, after breakfast, Grandma used to comb out her waist length silver hair standing in front of the living room furnace, completely nude. Her finely wrinkled, saggy, purplish-veined body turned to and fro, exposing front and back to anyone and everyone who happened to be in the room, even our brothers.

Debby and I were uncertain what to do. Our mothers never suggested we sleep with our fathers. And my mother was modest. She jumped as though buck naked if I came upon her unexpectedly, though she always wore foundation garments, stockings, and over all this a full slip. I had never seen her naked. However, the night *was* a little cold. I considered this as we slowly brushed our teeth. Through the door, I could see Grandpa already had on his pajamas.

When we entered the bedroom, he was in the center of the bed, under the covers. The nurses of Grandma's graduating class stared out from the photograph beside the dresser, and a large framed print—a florid painting of foxes, owls, and raccoons with big eyes—looked straight at us as we crossed the room and got into the bed, one to the left and one to the right of Grandpa. I was closest to the door. Straight as an arrow, arms to my side, I breathed as quietly as possible. Debby was likely doing the same.

Grandpa reached over and took my hand. Then he moved my hand across his thigh and placed it on some warm skin, his other hand, I guessed. But then, the warm skin changed, it moved. This was not a hand! I leapt up and bounded into the living room and lay on the sofa, wrapping myself tightly in an afghan. Nausea and dizziness consumed me in the near dark as I counted my breaths to keep my mind and my heart shut from what happened. Eventually, I fell asleep.

It was still dark, but less so, when I heard a noise. Awakening, I discovered Grandpa leaning over me. He quickly lay over me with all his weight. I was pinned down, wrapped tight in the wool afghan as he scratched my face with his rough whiskers.

Wet saliva covered my cheek as I turned my face into the sofa, away. I began to cry, struggling to push him off. When I cried louder, he went away. Back to the bedroom, where Debby was.

First thing next morning, we called our parents and asked them to come and get us. We cleaned up the kitchen, packed our things, and waited outside next to the knobby pine. We did not speak to him, did not speak of the night. From that day forward he was not Grandpa. To me my step-grandfather was a nonentity. A nothing. I did not look at him nor speak to him, unless absolutely necessary. He ceased to exist. But my guilt at leaving my cousin alone with him remained.

In a couple of months Debby got a golden palomino. Tending to her big gelding in the broad meadow beside her house was her focus now. No more spy trips, no more days at the river, no more trips to Grandma's. Debby rode the trails on the hills above Placerville with her new best friend, Sunshine. I remained in the canyon, alone.

NINE

How to Be Human, 1963

Wild all through the year, the South Fork of the American River rose and fell seasonally. One day when was twelve, I sat alone on a gravel bar surrounded by a clutter of random stones and noticed no rock was exactly like another. Each had grainy gray or white speckles. Some stones were very big, some tiny, yet all were tumbled smooth and nearly round. I lay across the sun-warmed rocks under the high blue sky. Watching a hazy cloud drift above, I imagined the journey that brought the rocks there, swept downstream with the high water in winter. One day they might be worn all the way down to fine sand. Everything on the Earth, including me, was bound to change. But sometimes change was so slow it was imperceptible.

While drowsing on the rocks, my eye was drawn to a strange brownish lump, some kind of nest bending low a branch of yellow Scotch broom. Almost immediately, a brilliant red-orange blast of color sprayed out and up, a firework of ladybugs hatching! In less than a minute the hundreds, maybe thousands, of shiny, tiny bugs were gone. Only the slight swaying of the branch, which now stood taller, gave proof they were ever there.

On another day, a giant swarm of monarch butterflies descended, a delirium of delicate black and orange-gold. Landing beside me on the beach, their wings closed and opened slowly, in chorus, as they silently sipped moisture from the damp sand. Like the ladybugs, they left as suddenly as they appeared.

I could count on the natural world to bestow a sense of belonging. People, however, were unreliable, confounding, and sometimes dangerous. Yet here I was. A person. I could never be a lizard or a ladybug or a butterfly. Was there a way to combine lessons from nature with the inevitability of being human?

On the walk home after school each day, I passed a lone pine standing arrow straight, bristling with sharp needles. After a rain, the tree looked fresh and bright, but even when the needles were dusty and dry, the tree stood proud, fully present. No shame. I called this "treeing." Stars starred; rivers river-ed. This was nature. At a bend in the road, a single oak clutched the hillside beside a seasonal waterfall. On one side of the oak's muscular trunk grew a tremendous fungus, layers of golden, fuzzy folds.

As I passed the giant fungus each day, I politely averted my eyes. The fungus was unseemly, right? Then one day it came to me. If the waterfall is sparkling and the tree is treeing, surely the fungus is simply fungus-ing. All around me life was unfolding. The essence of each element of nature was demonstrated. Look at the moon, the stars, rocks, baby ferns, sparkling water. Everything shared its essence without undue fret, without shame. I wondered—could people do this? Could I?

I left the road to sit on the beach and glided my hand in a slow swirl through the warm, fine sand beside me. What makes *people* unique? We move freely around. We invent things. We communicate with words. Could these qualities be the key to peopling?

The sand cooled, the shadow of the canyon wall crept closer, the sun dropped below the rim. I thought about all I learned from nature: suchness, acceptance, belonging. Gratitude. What if we were here, as people, to share the joy of being alive? Could it be that simple?

Caring, sensing, sharing: these would be the foundation of my philosophy. I would go out into the world and "display fascination with the life process." *This* was *my* way to be human.

Sensitivity

I knew this word as a criticism—that is, "too sensitive." But a different kind of sensitivity, the positive kind, would be the cornerstone of my theory on how to be human. My heart pounded double time as I hurried home. There was a new clarity to the air around me, a tenderness in the fading sunlight.

In my room I got out fresh paper, a good pen, and essays from the back page of two *Time* magazines. I revised and rewrote my theory until I was ready to commit to every word and every phrase. Then, in my best penmanship, I made one clean two-page copy. Across the top of my essay, the title: *Sensitivity*. The first person I wanted to share this with? Dr. Williams, my mother's therapist. Then I would submit the essay to *Time*.

My mother started seeing Dr. Williams right after we moved to the river. Dad's version of riverfront life dictated our nights and weekends: lots of drinks, lots of jokes, and lots of people. He invited friends and customers for swimming and barbeque every weekend and sometimes after work too. My parents loved to dance, but trips to Lake Tahoe, Sacramento, and San Francisco were rare now. Dad was much too busy in his paradise. Soon my mother started classes toward a master's degree in psychology, and education became her escape.

Mom's studying was a private affair, managed when we were at school or late at night. She kept the house running as usual and served dinner on time while commuting two hours each day.

She began seeing the therapist, Dr. Williams, at his office near the college.

Before long Mom decided we three kids would go to Dr. Williams, "for IQ testing." I suspect there was more to it than that. At my first session, Williams asked me to describe my family. After thinking a bit, I said, "Imagine each of us lives on a separate island in the sea. On each island there is a rowboat, with oars. But so far, no one has ever rowed to anyone else's island."

From time to time my mother would "haul us off to that quack," as my father put it. We were surprised when she got my father to go on his own. According to Dad, only fifteen minutes into the session Dr. Williams said, "Well, Joe, I am not sure how I can help you."

"See, what did I tell you? Williams says I don't need therapy," Dad said at dinner that night, lifting his bourbon in a toast to himself.

I told Dr. Williams I planned to be a writer, and he mentioned a school in Iowa that was famous for teaching writing. The day I brought my essay to him, I chose my outfit with care—a cranberry wool skirt, cranberry sweater, and deep red Capezio shoes. Before leaving the house, I checked the mirror, searching for a sign of wisdom. My brown eyes looked not just brown but like tiger-eye agate, as though lit from within. In the waiting room I held my essay by the edges; my hands were sweating. I had never shared anything so personal, and so profound, with another person.

When I entered the office, Dr. Williams was at his desk. A prissy middle-aged man, he always wore high-waist gray slacks, a navy blazer, a white shirt, and a striped or patterned yellow tie. I handed my work across the desk and took a seat opposite. He looked up, put on his glasses, and read. When he put the pages down, he looked at me from above his glasses, then took them off.

I waited.

"Well, Elisa, this is very well written. Where did you copy it from?" he asked as he pushed my essay back across the desk.

Appalled, I could not speak at first. I stammered a few lines, trying to explain my scientific method, but he cut me off.

"You evidently read these concepts somewhere and put them together in your own words, but this is certainly not *your* work."

In an instant, my pride and hope were transmuted to anger, then armor. I was done with him. Dr. Williams was dust.

I was so offended I could hardly speak.

I blinked a few times, took a breath, and though I was crushed, I refused to let on.

I never submitted the essay to a magazine, never shared it with teachers or adults. My theory of how to be human was a private treasure, a gift from the canyon, mined one nugget at a time.

Only the river knew the real me.

TEN

A Spirit Door, 1963

n eighth grade, the gifted program started up at our school, and on Saturdays I went to a special class at the high school. The college sociology professor teaching the class looked a little like Leonard Cohen and lectured with a wry smile, as though he had deep insights. He started us out with Orwell's *Animal Farm*, and soon I realized he expected us to think. To question. To speak up. Even the girls!

"Miss Stancil, what is the author telling us here? Is there more to the story than we see on the page? Is there a parallel here between the society on the farm and our society?"

I participated in class as though at a feast, a banquet of unimaginable opportunity. I read and pondered every page, prepared questions in advance. Saturday class was where I belonged. After Orwell, we read *Lord of the Flies*.

One night I overheard Dad on the phone. He called the professor a "Commie Jew." Placerville was provincial, and my father was biased. When the semester ended, there were no more Saturday classes. Now plain old Placerville would forever be too limiting, too suppressing—not just for my mother, but for me.

When national magazines featured articles on Sister Mary Corita, an antiwar activist and nun, I was struck by her artwork. Her serigraphs and posters had snippets of words mixed with calligraphy, almost childlike—E. E. Cummings meets Matisse. My favorite? "I greet the light in you." These few words, rendered in her unique stick-printing style and accompanied by a blue, torn-paper bird in flight, created a spirit door, an opening . . . an idea. Why stay in Placerville? Could I find a *school* like Saturday class, where girls were whole people and art was alive?

Sister Mary Corita taught at a Catholic girls' school in Southern California, but there was another Catholic boarding school in Belmont, just south of San Francisco: Notre Dame High School for Girls. I sent for a brochure. Mom was all for it. Surely her own girlhood would have turned out differently if she had been able to go to a progressive boarding school.

"Why in the hell do you want to go to that nunnery?" was Dad's first question. I brushed this off. There *were* three hundred nuns at Notre Dame, sure, but also eight hundred day students and one hundred boarders. When at last he agreed to tour the place, he reserved a suite for us in an expensive San Francisco hotel. We had an early dinner in a pricey restaurant with dark paneled wood. My parents hardly talked that night; when they did, they sounded stilted. The weekend was intended as a tribute, a signal from my parents that I was embarking on something special.

We went to see Mary Martin in *South Pacific*, and Mom laughed openly as Mary Martin "washed that man" out of her hair. The musical, rich with sounds and sights, temporarily filled the emptiness between us. "Let's have a drink," Dad said when we returned to the hotel, opening his arms expansively and taking a half turn at the window as he looked out at the city lights. "No, Joe, not tonight," Mom said. I closed the door to my room.

When Monday came, Dad wore a dark suit. Mom donned her favorite fitted tweed dress, a hat, and short gloves. I picked a butter-colored mohair sweater and matching skirt. We fit together like an ideal American family. You'd never know we were from some canyon miles outside a hick town like Placerville. At the school, my parents filled out the application while I took a long aptitude test.

The patina on the old plaster buildings, the eucalyptus groves, and the shady paths matched pictures in the brochure. We walked the grounds with one of the nuns and toured one of the large dormitories. The cubicles and narrow wooden closets looked simple and plain, reminding me of Grandma Bishop's house. After the tour, Mother Superior ushered us into her sunny office and crossed the room to welcome me to the school. I had scored high on the test. I was in.

Before we left, we toured the art studio in the half basement beneath the gym. There, Sister Mary Corita's posters filled one whole wall. The worktables were cluttered with bright collages, works in progress. In the hall stood a row of girls' bikes, ready to ride throughout the high school and adjoining college campus. This was just what I was looking for, a place where I could be who I was on the inside, out in a big world, a place to be safe and free.

A few weeks later, Mom and I drove to San Francisco to shop at the City of Paris department store. Under the giant stained-glass dome, our perfumed sales lady spread the school's uniform across a gleaming marble counter. Her manicure shone as she primly straightened the plain white blouse, the sweater, the box-pleated skirt, and short, square jacket. I looked on and my heart sank.

"Is this, um, everything?" I asked.

"This is the uniform for all the girls at your school, my dear. There are no other pieces."

Oh ... brown and yellow. I'd expected at least a plaid skirt. Maybe grosgrain ribbon on the placket of the yellow sweater? But no.

In the bright dressing room I tried everything on and, turning to the mirror, saw what I feared: a square, itchy me. My cheeks already felt rashy from the wool, and the color was what I later came to call, as a colorist, an "unfortunate brown." Mom bought one skirt, one jacket, one sweater, and two blouses, though the lady said, "Students buy a minimum of two sets of everything, of course."

"Yes," my mother replied, looking at the price tags. "We'll take two blouses, and one of everything else. We need to be sure it works out before we buy more."

Works out? Why would it not work out?

Fragmented by suppressed panic, I zigzagged through the fancy store carting my new clothes. What was I doing? Nobody in my town went away to high school, not even the boys. Would I be able to match the polish, the burnish, and the heft of my new life? Maybe *I* was too plain, too small town. Maybe the uniform looked right on the right girls.

On the long drive home, whatever Mom and I could have shared about the future, the past, or even the truth of that very moment never materialized. We pretended to be fine, continuing our long-standing tacit agreement to share with one another no information, no fears, and no hopes. If you *act* fine, you will be treated as though you *are* fine. This pretense, enacted by so many women and girls in my world in 1963, was like a glass mountain. There was no way to get any traction once this pretense was in place.

Summer passed slowly with babysitting jobs, long weekends on the river, tanning on Dad's raft, barbeques with people from Dad's work and relatives from town. All the while my impending departure loomed. Excitement gave way to sentimental interludes as September approached. Meanwhile there was something happening with Tommy. Now he sat beside me if we were sunning on rocks after a swim. He brought me an ice cream without my asking. I caught him looking at me when he thought I didn't see. Maybe I was growing up enough to be a girlfriend. But what did that mean, really?

The moonless night before I left for boarding school, it happened. Tommy shepherded me out onto the deck without a word. My heart was beating hard, and I could hardly see his face. I felt awkward with his arm around me, even though I wanted closeness. When he bent to kiss me, it felt as heavy as wet sand, somehow lifeless. I turned away just a bit and waited, wanting it to end.

I have no way of knowing if residue from my step-grandfather factored into my experience that night. I just knew that despite my fervent imaginings, I was not quite ready for a *real* boyfriend. If I had stayed in Placerville, we might have flowed naturally into romance, but at thirteen and sixteen, after years of friendship, we were unable that night to manage anything poetic.

There's a business term used when comparing costs of a project. The difference between the lowest bid and the highest price a client is willing to pay is a measurement called the "delta." When I was packing to leave for Notre Dame, the delta between the worst thing that might happen if I stayed home in Placerville and the best if I excelled while away seemed too great to measure.

In the natural world, wild spring rivers run fast and high, pulling sediment from the banks and carrying it along toward a curve or a valley where the current slows enough to leave the silt behind. Over time, layers of silt and sediment form deltas that look peaceful, broad, and sleepy. In fact, they're a record of the raging currents that created them. We all live somewhere in our own deltas, bounded by both our deepest fears and our greatest expectations. By this point, my delta was so broad it seemed to have its own horizon.

ELEVEN

Unintended Consequences, 1963

The day my parents took me to boarding school, I kept an eye out for Mother Superior, just to say hello. In the rush of families, I didn't see her anywhere. We found my assigned dorm cubicle, next to the hall door. No sun reached the little curtained space, but we weren't allowed in the dorm during the day anyway. There was a narrow bed, a tall dresser, and one stiff chair, with just enough room between the bed and dresser to change clothes. I quickly arranged my single uniform and jumble of personal stuff in the closet, stacking my tennis shoes, slippers, and seven colorful pairs of Capezio flats on the bottom shelf.

Once all was arranged, I acted offhand, like starting my new life was no big deal. Dad was not his usual brash self; he paced without a word, jangling the change in his pockets. Mom had tears in her eyes; her back was stiff and straight.

"Would you like to walk us back to the car?" she asked.

"No, just go now," was all I said. Coming here had been my idea; how would it look if I started to cry?

As soon as they left, I was on the move, heading for the art studio in hopes of overriding the feeling of hollowness caused by their departure. In the quiet, low hall of the half-underground basement, a small nun abruptly signaled me to a halt, silently holding her palm flat in the air between us. Her eyes—framed by the rigid, white wimple of the Carmelite order—were a commanding rich brown rimmed with dark lashes. This nun was a natural beauty.

"Good afternoon, Sister, I am looking for the art studio," I said quietly. With pursed lips and controlled gestures, she directed me without a word, then whirled in a tidy, practiced arabesque. Her rosary beads quietly clacked against the folds of her full-length habit as she strode away.

The art studio was dark, locked up tight. And there stood the row of bicycles, chained together now, also locked. The tires were flat. My hopes began to deflate right then, one hour after I'd coolly dismissed my parents.

Had I made a mistake?

In the few months between my initial interview and the first day of school, the administration had undergone a regime change. Sister Marie Damien, the nun in the basement, was now Mother Superior and focused like a laser on comportment, religion, and prayer. We sometimes woke to our dorm nun signaling silence—an unscheduled day of silent retreat. Other days we were required to wear white gloves, but no one said why. Sister Marie Damien was my grandmother incarnate; silence and white gloves were her scrub brush and bleach.

When I dared ask where Sister Mary Corita had gone, where I might write her, my homeroom nun said only, "Oh, well dear, Sister Corita taught in Los Angeles." Corita's fame in the early-to mid-1960s challenged the church. Her art and its message of peace and equality met with backlash. Now, at Notre Dame High School, Sister Marie Damien intended to scrub out creativity and free thinking altogether.

At this high school, all my classmates had strong test scores. If I'd stayed in Placerville, I could have skipped general science and freshman English, but here I was nothing more than average. This was daunting. In study hall I filled my notebook with poems and sketches, memories of my river.

There was no time for real nature unless you counted the hour of water ballet in the heavily chlorinated indoor pool. I learned, after much practice, to hold my breath, hook my toes under the armpits of the girl floating on her back just ahead of me as the girl behind me did the same to me. We used our arms to move in unison, a giant underwater wheel. As each of us ten girls took turns skimming the surface, we had time for one breath before we were pulled below again. The whole semester was like this giant underwater wheel; I was starving for breath, forced to comply with a world that was as suspect and foreign as the dense chapters in our religion book.

Nearly every night I heard girls crying in the dark, and from the far corner I thought I sometimes heard the dorm nun's quiet tears too. I refused to cry. Instead I illicitly read and reread *Gone with the Wind*, using a small brass clip-on light to illuminate Scarlett O'Hara's Phoenix-like saga. By the end of the semester I'd read it at least nine times, although the nuns impounded my book light and radio more than once. When these were returned after a week, the batteries were dead. Clearly the nuns were using my radio and light themselves. After the third time, I told the dorm nun, "Sister, if you need your own radio, I can arrange to get you one, but please stop wearing down my batteries." Without a word the nun departed, my radio still in hand.

I was not fitting in at boarding school but to admit this was to concede defeat. Returning to Placerville was unthinkable after deeming my local high school sub par.

None of the teachers at Notre Dame were as electric and

inspiring as the Saturday school professor my father called "that Commie Jew." And my imaginary mentor, Sister Mary Corita, was unreachable. My quest to expand my world had instead collapsed it. Without the comfort of nature, whatever tender understanding I had of life was unreachable as well.

Classmates were little help. At night some of the older popular girls climbed out the window and crossed two roofs to a fire escape to meet up with their boyfriends. The unsure girls like me fell into a couple of categories: afraid and sad, or afraid and angry. I was angry.

Beginning the first week and continuing every few weeks, pair after pair of my Capezios disappeared from my closet. I tried to get a lock for my closet but was refused. No nuns wanted to confront the fact that girls were stealing, I guess. After the third pair disappeared, I held a loud protest, yelling that the thief or thieves should return the shoes. "Think about it. You are never going to be able to wear them around here." No shoes were returned.

During the war, my mother was stationed for a while near Florence, Italy, where she bought a pendant made of fine silver filigree and tiny diamonds. In the center, a carved disc of milky mother of pearl depicted the Madonna and child. This carving was so discreet, the image was discernible only when lit from an angle, like a silent prayer. The day before I left for school, my mother quietly offered me this amulet, which symbolized so much that remained unsaid between us.

One morning another angry girl from my dorm walked by—with my mother's necklace on. She must have taken it from my dresser drawer. When confronted, she called me a liar. In an instant, my primitive core overheated, and I grabbed her, dragged her across the hall into the white-tiled bathroom, and pressed her face against the window overlooking the garden two stories below. Pinning her there with her cheek pressed hard against the glass, one hand on her throat, I put my face close to hers.

"Take my necklace off now, you lying bitch, or I *will* throw you out this window."

When I came out of the bathroom I had my necklace.

On my first trip home, I wrote poems in the San Francisco bus terminal. One likened my time at school to gray pigeons pecking at crumbs in the fading light. After wadding it up and tossing it in the trash, I fished it out and pressed it between the pages of my book in case I did become famous someday, which seemed more and more unlikely. All the way home, rereading *Gone with the Wind*, I studied Scarlett and prepared to pretend everything was fine.

When I arrived, exhausted from the slow bus trip, I was eager to see my old Dalmatian, Duchess, and my cats. But Jiggs confronted me the moment I walked into the house.

"Duchess and all those cats of yours, well, they're dead, now," he said with little expression.

"What? What are you saying?" I stammered.

"Well, Duchess had arthritis, so Dad said I had to shoot her. He said just dig a hole out on a sand bank and put a bowl of food next to it and as soon as she gets eating it good, shoot her in the back of the head. When she falls in the hole, it's easy to bury her."

Jiggs dug the hole but couldn't bring himself to shoot. My father grabbed the gun and shot Duchess point blank. My two cats had fourteen kittens while I was away, and they were relegated to the woodpile out back where they became weekend target practice for my brother and Debby's older brother, Craig. Craig had shot Debby's cat the year before while she was at music camp, so this elimination of pets was not unheard of. But it was brutal.

Everything at home seemed surreal. In the morning I looked

for my bicycle, ready to ride it down the long driveway to the bridge and back to smooth out my anxiety. Where could it be?

"You left your bike when you went away to your fancy school," Dad said, "and your brother is using it now." Jiggs built a homemade motorcycle and used my blue cruiser for parts. In four weeks my bike and all my pets had been erased. Clearly no one at home was concerned with my wellbeing.

TWELVE

Subterranean, 1964

At Notre Dame, CeCe roomed at the opposite end of our dorm, and, though she was a year older, we started hanging out together. There was an unexplored intersection between my resentment of the school's regime change and CeCe's despair over the recent death of her mother. We were both angry and feeling powerless. Her father traveled for business, so though her home was nearby, she was now a boarder instead of a day student. Sometimes we'd go to CeCe's house and sneak her mother's aqua T-bird convertible out for a drive. CeCe drove with her tan legs crossed, her left foot on the gas like some kind of movie star, as we toured town with the top down, smoking cigarettes and listening to Martha and the Vandellas.

CeCe was the first pampered, upper-middle-class girl I knew. Her father let her have anything. With golden streaks added to her light brown hair, tawny unfreckled skin, and an already curvy shape, she looked at least eighteen. If you didn't know better, you would assume she was carefree. But all she had once taken for granted was in question, and her life was in the midst of a tremendous change, much like mine. We almost never discussed this. Instead, we spent time off campus looking for boys and critiquing the nuns and girls. We tried pot one time, but the smoke was harsh, dry, and hot. I itched and then felt sleepy and stupid. When we got back to the dorm, I had a heavy headache that lasted for hours.

I studied less and less, and my grades dropped.

A few weeks later, I returned home for the second time. The house was silent; my brothers and father were out swimming. Mom called me into the kitchen.

"Elisa, I have something serious to talk to you about," she said. But then she didn't say anything. She just stood there, wooden.

"Is Dad dying?" I asked. "Are you dying?" Maybe what happened to CeCe would happen to me. Whatever was going on, I could tell it was serious by Mom's tone.

"No, it's nothing like that . . . your father and I are getting a divorce."

Her face was gray and still. She didn't move, didn't reach out or even uncross her arms. I spun away and ran to my room and stood beside my curtains, leaning into the fabric. I pressed my cheek against a bit of cool window glass, trying to think. In a few seconds, I realized this news was a kind of relief. They were not happy together as far as I could tell. Why should they stay married? No need to be dramatic about it, right?

Back in the kitchen, Mom was still standing there by herself.

"Whatever you do, I will support you," I told her quietly, thinking this was probably what Scarlett O'Hara would say. I would stand by in emergencies. And if I didn't, who would?

"I just can't stay married anymore," Mom said, looking away. "There's no one else involved."

Someone else?

"I'll go back to nursing," she continued. "You kids will stay with me. We might move down to the Bay Area after I find a job. Everything will be okay."

I felt sick to my stomach and went to my room to lie down. Would I have to quit Notre Dame? Would I care if I did? That afternoon, Tommy's father Karl showed up by himself. Besides being my father's accountant, Karl was a short-story writer. For the past couple of years he had read his work aloud to Mom in our kitchen down by the river in the afternoons. Mom said Karl wanted to take me for a drive.

I was surprised; we had never gone anywhere alone before. Maybe he wanted to talk to me about a letter I'd sent to Tommy a couple of weeks before, with an E. E. Cummings poem about the future walking on little cat's feet. I'd hand-lettered the lines on stiff watercolor paper using Sister Corita's stick-printing style and painted two blue birds on one side.

Karl was jittery. He opened the passenger door for me like I was a grownup woman. When he turned down a back road, I began calculating what might happen if I jumped out of the car at this speed. Was he planning to molest me? I put my hand on the door handle, but just then he pulled over and parked. I was about to leap out when he put a hand on my arm and, turning toward me, said in a most sincere tone, "I hope you know I will always be very good to your mother."

Oh. My. God. Karl, with his bald head, his wooden leg, his thick waist, his kind ways. Karl, the intellectual who wrote short stories, was in love with my mother. And Mom, the depressed and lonely woman buried in a canyon, had chosen Karl as her escape route. Tommy, my almost boyfriend, was about to become my stepbrother.

As soon as Karl dropped me off, I confronted my mother. "You lied! And now you are turning my boyfriend into my *stepbrother*?"

"What are you talking about?" Mom kept her voice low. "You never said Tommy was your boyfriend." She raised no defense about lying.

When I checked in with my brothers, Jiggs was cleaning a revolver. "I am gonna kill Karl if I see him," he said, through clenched teeth.

Ed, who was only eleven, was setting up a miniature steam engine in his bedroom. He loved machinery, especially taking it apart, and was trying very hard to put the disassembled replica of a working steam engine back together.

"Look, Ed, no matter what we wish was going on, we have to admit Mom and Dad are not happy together, right?" I tried to catch his eye as he fiddled with the machine. I could see his shoulders rise and fall as he let out a long sigh.

"Yeah, but where will we live? Why does everything have to fall apart?" he asked. When he looked my way, he had tears in his eyes. "And what about Dad?"

"I don't have any answers right now. Let's try not to make anything worse. Keep an eye on Jiggs, okay?" I gathered my stuff and pestered Jiggs for a ride to the Greyhound bus station.

I headed back to Notre Dame on the first bus out. I leaned against the window and watched the landscape stream by. My life as I knew it was being dismantled, piece by piece.

A few days after the alarming news about Karl and my mother, a half-page letter arrived from Tommy. He included sketches of race cars, an offering beyond my power to interpret. He asked to visit me at Notre Dame.

In the dorm preparing for his visit, I plucked my eyebrows for the first time, but they looked uneven, and by the time I finished, there were almost none left. To compensate, I borrowed some foundation from CeCe, but it was too harsh and somehow made me look angry. I anxiously scrubbed it away. There was great weight to this meeting, hours away from Placerville, without my brothers, without our parents or the reflected light of summer. Who were we now?

When Tommy arrived, he seemed to have lost his lanky comfort, his casual confidence. He looked down a lot and hardly said a word. I, too, said almost nothing. We were not ourselves. We were out of our depth.

We sat uncomfortably on the stiff settee in a glassed-in room and had no words. The nuns would not permit us to go out under the giant eucalyptus trees where swaying chains of little leaves whispered like a distant river. They wouldn't allow me to walk Tommy to the door and stand in the weak winter sun for a moment, unobserved.

When I called home, Jiggs told me that Mom and Karl had run off together to a cabin in Reno so Mom could get a quick divorce. Dad dispatched Ivan Ivanoff, his bill collector, to confront them. Ivan, a rugged foreigner, rumored to have been a freedom fighter in Bulgaria, fled the war in his home country by hiding in a pond in the dark of night, along with his family and other townspeople. Ivan's wife was critically wounded when the water was sprayed with German bullets, and, complying with a desperate agreement among the townspeople in the pond, Ivan was forced to drown his wife to stifle her cries. He took a bullet in his thigh but managed to crawl out and away. Some years later, he arrived in Placerville and began working for my father.

Brandishing a pistol, Ivan knocked on the door of the cabin in Reno.

"That weasel Karl practically peed himself," Jiggs relayed with satisfaction. "Mom is back home now." Using Ivan as his stealthy knight, Dad had won the final chess match with Karl.

Mom returned to the canyon and resumed her studies with grim acquiescence. Tommy and Karl disappeared from Placerville without a trace.

The next time I returned home there was increased tension and even less conversation. Dad joined my mother each night in the silent living room and sat studying school lessons in his favorite Danish modern chair by the fire. He had promised Mom he would get his high school diploma.

In November, we learned the river would be dammed. Dad had done all he could to stop it, but a hydroelectric plant was being built a mile and a half upstream from our house. Water would be released on some kind of hydroelectric schedule, and the tamed river would run cold all through the summer.

One morning over Thanksgiving break, I looked out my window and saw Dad standing alone in the driveway beside his truck, tears on his face. I had never seen my father rendered powerless. I knew then this was goodbye to paradise. Goodbye to our custom-built raft with the chrome ladder anchored in the swimming hole. Goodbye to Dad's barbeques, his chance to share drinks and crass humor with various hangers-on out on the deck as the sun went down. Goodbye to floating the rapids without a tube, exploring the inlets under the shore willows on sunny afternoons.

I stepped away from the window. Granting my father privacy was the only comfort I could think to give him.

Back at boarding school, I went to the nurse in the evenings complaining of a stomachache or headache. Her warm office was next to the cafeteria, and she gave me cookies and milk. Sometimes she even rubbed my back. I gained twenty pounds.

At the end of the semester, the nuns informed me I was being expelled. I felt ashamed and humiliated, even though I hated it there. When I learned the reason given, I was horrified. There, on the letter to my parents, I read that I was expelled for "pseudo sophistication." What did this even mean?

I should have left the very first week, when I knew the school would not deliver creative, challenging opportunities. Dad would have been happy to save the tuition.

"There's a perfectly good school in town, paid for by our taxes, you know," he said a number of times.

I could handle the family fallout, but I dreaded facing my former classmates. I had left them cold, judging Placerville a hick town without merit for a genius like me. I felt nauseated at the prospect of facing everyone in town.

My parents collected my few remaining shoes, my personal belongings, and me. I left my single uniform hanging in the closet.

At home, the dam a mile and a half upstream was already underway.

AFTER THE FIRE,
WINTER 2018

After the fire, a fresh peeled rawness persisted in Glen Ellen. When the village market and bar reopened, neighbors gathered. Old greetings like, "How are you doing?" were too painful to bear. Simple nods sufficed. The community rose up, and donations of goods and money were collected and shared. What to do, how to do, when to do? Answers were sketchy for those with losses and those with none.

Letting go happens in stages. After deep loss, these stages can be waves, riptides, tsunamis, or a steady drizzle of gloom. Down the lanes all around our town where houses once stood, burned-out lots were dotted with twisted, melted cars, exposed chimneys, and stone steps leading nowhere. Over all this, the first winter rain fell like tears.

Fire survivors Claudia, a filmmaker, and Erick, a sculptor and assemblage artist, responded right away to our posting about the Twill House. They had lost their rental home, his sculpture studio and equipment, her computers and cameras, all materials for both their careers, both vehicles, and all their possessions. Alerted by a neighbor the night of the fire, they could only save themselves. They had lost everything but the will to rebuild and the ability to trust that they would.

When we met to discuss sharing the land with them, I heard myself repeat one phrase a number of times—mutually beneficial. In fact, their very presence could be a balm for me. Sharing was a small act of penance after failing to hail our neighbors during the firestorm.

I hoped the Twill House could be a source of healing for them. What some would call discomforts, like the composting toilet and outdoor shower, these artists saw as benefits. Our horses and proximity to thousands of acres of wild land reminded them of the place they had lost, and offered gentle peace and privacy.

They carted boxes and bags of donated clothes in the wheelbarrow, down the path to the furnished Twill House. Erick reorganized the basement, removed a half-century's worth of cobwebs, and constructed a temporary studio. Claudia continued her work as a grant manager for nonprofits, putting her filmmaking and dance projects on hold while she got her bearings. They grieved there in the little house and waited for spring.

Meanwhile, rain fell, and an even mist floated over the hillsides across the valley. In this chill I turned inward, thinking about self-reliance and recovery. Early experiences, and the beliefs I created around them, had inadvertently armored me. What would it take to melt this unintended consequence?

THIRTEEN

Trying to Make It Real, 1964–1965

When I returned after one semester at boarding school, a rumor spread through the local high school. "Elisa never went away to a fancy school. She left to have a baby, and she gave it away." This was probably based on my weight gain and short absence, no doubt exacerbated by Placerville's low expectations of girls. Without a clear source and no real way to counter it, I let it float.

To gain some ground, I decided to start a girls' track team. Running always set my mind right. Five other girls—good runners with wins from outlying elementary schools—agreed to join. I set up a meeting with the principal. The principal's tendency to suppress change was a concern. After all, he banned *Animal Farm* and suspended the Saturday sociology classes I loved so much. But this was sport.

In his office, I listed the girls who were interested and included our impressive middle school sprinting and cross-country times. Two neighboring high schools already had girls' teams, though in 1964 there was no such thing as Title IX. He said he would get back to me within a week.

A few days later he sat at his desk as he laid out his ideas for the team.

"I know you girls want to be involved, and I've talked it over with the PE department. We have a plan we think you're going to like. You girls can have your own little uniforms," he counted off on his fingers, ". . . your own little clipboards, even your own stopwatches."

He saw me looking at him skeptically and made a stab at clinching the deal.

"You girls can keep the boys' times!" His benevolent smile dissolved when he saw the shock on my face.

"Well now, Elisa," he stammered. "We all know the real reason you girls want to be out there is to be with the boys . . ." He finished his smarmy pitch, still selling. "We even thought of a name. You could be the *Trackettes*."

My face flushed hot, as though I had been slapped. "We want to *run*, not be timekeepers. We want to *run*."

Another clever vision turned to dust. Placerville was stuck in the past, and now I was too.

Back at the river, the water ran cold all summer even in the heat of the day. The new dam bridged the canyon, and now the regulated flow, released from the huge new lake, came from the cold depths. In a single day, the level of the river might change four times, running low, then high, then somewhere between. All shore life was gone within weeks: the lumpy ladybug nests, tiny water snakes and blinking newts, the minnows, the Monarch butterflies fluttering in huge swarms to sip water from the sand. All gone.

I stayed inside and began to read beside my mother in our chilled house, anything and everything—all of John Updike, most of Dostoyevsky, what I could find of Sinclair Lewis and Thomas Mann, Voltaire, Aristophanes, along with a few failed attempts at Shakespeare.

Dr. Williams had said that at fourteen I was too young to understand the complex human interactions in these books. What was the big deal? People struggling to get along, to get what they want with varying degrees of success. At least there was humor in *Candide,* and *Madame Bovary* had the same issues as my mother. *Babbitt?* That character *was* my dad, a man disillusioned with middle-class life, stymied by societal rules. Compared to literature, the life I was living beside the dead river was empty. Not gritty. There was nothing to dig into, nothing to build on. Any tepid friendships I had at the high school cooled further now that there was no chance to swim in the icy river. I was bored.

After a few months of dieting, I'd lost most of my Notre Dame weight. My future as a famous writer and artist appeared to be on hold, so I tried on different identities. There were not many options in my small town. I considered getting a boyfriend. At high school no one compared with Tommy, but Tommy was no more.

Like a strong, sweet tea, my romantic ideas were steeped in the pages of books like *Ramona, My Antonia,* and *Gone with the Wind.* I craved belonging and tenderness, not actual sex.

I imagined someone strong, someone funny, someone durable. A companion. At a town dance not long after, I heard a girl laughing and watched as she was carried high through the crowd. All heads turned as she was carted out the door. Who was her powerful He-Man? Could he be mine?

Ron was his name. He was a football star, a giant boy, impish and brutish all at once. He walked with a bit of a lope mid-stride and cracked clever jokes, followed by a shy smile. All physical things came easily to Ron, yet he seemed almost apologetic for his grace and power. His family was disadvantaged, his dad crippled in a mill accident years before. Everyone in town knew Ron's scrawny older brother was wild, people said he was addicted to benzidrene. His older sister Norma married at sixteen and had three kids by the time she was twenty. Of them all, Ron was the golden one. He was going to graduate from high school—and he played football. He was funny and gleefully strong. I decided I liked him. By the end of my sophomore year, much to my parents' chagrin, Ron became my boyfriend.

"His parents don't have two nickels to rub together. What in the hell are you interested in him for?" my father said loudly at dinner, swirling his scotch and soda in one hand.

"Now, Joe . . ." my mother started, then said no more.

"He's fun and he likes me," was my retort. "Everything is not about money, you know."

"You say that now but wait until you're on your own someday. Then let's see what you have to say," Dad replied.

I stood to clear the table. Acting busy was a good way to end sticky conversations with my father.

The first time I met Ron's family, he and I climbed steep steps to the cluttered front porch of their rental house, hand in hand. In the dark living room, instead of curtains, the windows had cheap, dusty pull-down roller shades stuck at haphazard angles partway between open and closed.

Ron's mother, Kate, wearing shaggy slippers and an apron over a loose housedress, took my hand in greeting, then closed in for a half hug, with a laugh. This was her day off. Kate was short and meaty. She was to her family what my father was to mine— the power, the blood. She worked as a cook most of her life, and at home she tossed together meals for five or twenty with an off-hand assurance, her Tareyton cigarette marking time like a loose baton. She brewed coffee in a big, dented aluminum percolator for the many people who visited on any given day. She was not in any way measured; she was not like my mother.

When I was fifteen, this woman was like a beacon, giving me hope for a comfortable, even *fun* womanhood. At Kate's, the worn, mismatched furniture stood in disarray, but nonetheless felt welcoming. In our house, carefully arranged Danish modern pieces rested on handloomed carpets. Kate tossed meat in a pan and made biscuits without a thought, while in our antiseptic kitchen, my mother double checked ingredients for recipes she had made a hundred times.

Ron took me to movies, to games, to pizza. Just before I turned sixteen, he implored me to have sex. I liked the idea of romance but was still immature. I'd had only had two periods, spaced a year apart.

Here was Ron. Should we have sex or not? I divided a piece of paper into two columns, pros/cons. After some thought, due to my limited knowledge, I concluded there was no halfway; either you had sex, or you didn't, right? What difference would it make if we just did it?

At the town pizza parlor where Debby worked after school and on weekends, Ron told me he had found a place for us to be together. As I studied the sweat on the outside of my cold Coke glass and listened to the nonsense song, "Woolly Bully," Ron placed a key on the table between us.

"What's that key?" I asked.

"This is Bob's grandma's house key. She lives on the golf course. She's in Hawaii, and Bob's taking care of her house."

"You told Bob?" I asked. Bob was on the football team, so everyone in town might already know where we were and what we were about to do.

"Nah, come on, I would never tell Bob. Geez, girl, give me some credit."

When we arrived at the silent house, I refused to step into the entry hall. This was trespassing. Instead, I suggested we go out on the golf course. It was dark, and no one was around; what difference did it make? Ron was fine with that. We fumbled through a three-minute experience, some of which hurt. We were somewhere in the rough, where the grass was scratchy. Then I was sticky, and there was a faint smell of bleach mixed with flowers.

Coaxing Ron to the swimming pool in Bob's grandmother's dark backyard, I rinsed off and swam alone in the lukewarm water, trying to feel grown up. I was ready to go back to the pizza place. Ron just stood naked on the second step of the pool, grinning his lopsided grin. I noted, not for the first time, how much his gracefully proportioned body resembled the statue of David. But anyhow, I was hungry. We had "done it." We could leave, right?

Minutes later I realized my error in thinking. He wanted to do it again. Maybe it was over too fast, we should do something different, and then we would be done?

Back to the grass, scratchy-scratchy-scratchy, my eyes squinched shut. Then he was done, pulling out at the last possible second. More bleachy scent. Back to the pool. A hiss of white noise, a dissonance blanketed me. I felt small and alone.

In my bedroom later I saw there was blood on my panties. I rinsed them clean and searched my eyes in the mirror, wondering if anyone could tell I was no longer a virgin. No, I looked the same.

On our very next date, instead of going to a friend's or to get something to eat, Ron drove down a dirt road and parked, then turned to me, and said, "Okay, let's get in the back."

It's not that he was gruff or rude or mean. He was just certain. This was where we were, in his world. But this was in neither of the two columns on the piece of paper where I'd calculated my fate. In that moment, I was like a primitive seeing the very first eclipse of the sun. Gray shadow spread over all my earth, leaving all I had known, all I was, diminished.

Down at the river, my little brother Ed had an ant farm in his room, a narrow block of sand compressed between two sheets of Plexiglas. The main colony never interested me for long. Busy ants made slow progress, downloading their data to each other every few steps, antennae wavering, front legs scribbling in the air. But sometimes a loner would set out on the virgin sand. In a few hours, maybe a day or two, a small outpost would be in full operation.

Once I surrendered my virginity, I saw no path back to my original colony. With a resigned sadness, I realized I had tunneled too far in my lone direction. I would have to build my own outpost.

FOURTEEN

Wishing and Hoping, 1966

My desire to belong, to feel connected, was like a magneto, a perpetual motion machine pushing me forward, overriding uncertainties that fluttered in the periphery. As a Catholic, I knew sex before marriage was a sin. I loved Ron more than I had ever loved anyone, right? Two more years of high school, followed by four years of college? Drudgery. Why wait to begin an independent, fulfilling life?

I prayed to the Virgin Mary to help me get pregnant. Then Ron and I could get married, and I would not be sinning. A simple win-win. Ron was informed of my plan. He didn't object. Prayer and sex worked wonders. Sitting near the train tracks on a back road outside of town a couple of months later, a fountain of light suddenly spread through the center of my body. Turning to Ron, I exclaimed, "Guess what? I'm pregnant!"

"What?" Ron stammered. "When did you go to the doctor?" To his credit, he believed me when I said, "I just found out. It happened just now, like a fountain inside." Over the next few weeks my breasts grew, I was sleepy and emotional. I began making lists of what we would need to outfit our apartment. We would build our own world.

When my parents found a note I had written to Ron, they realized I might be pregnant and whisked me off to their friend, a doctor in town. He met us in his office that evening. He examined me and confirmed I was about three months along. My parents immediately demanded I go to Mexico for an abortion. I refused, insisting Ron and I would marry. Ron's family concurred, but my father dismissed this.

"Of course. What do they care? They live off welfare. They think I'm going to be their gravy train."

That weekend we ran away, fifteen miles to his sister Norma's house. We surprised her as she was helping her husband cut venison from a fresh carcass hanging on their screened-in porch. Ron helped slice the fresh kill into long strips for the smoker, and night had fallen by the time he finished.

Ron's sister loaned us one sleeping bag, one pillow, and an old sheet. We cleared off a space on the floor of the porch off the kitchen and lay down. The cloying smells of raw venison and wood smoke seeped through the screen, through the sheet, into my long hair. Ron sprawled out, asleep, unaware.

By dawn my visions of a strong joyous family had shrunk, shriveling like the strips of jerky in the smoker. My "shortcut" agenda—just get pregnant, then get married—had steamrolled Ron. His hands trembled when he talked with Norma, so much so that he stuffed them in his pockets except when smoking her Tareytons.

"What in the hell is your plan?" Norma asked. "You can't stay here; we have a full house. You better figure something out, that's all I can say."

We had nowhere to go. No money. And Ron had no plan.

I returned to the river.

When Grandma Bishop called, insisting on meeting Ron, we felt relieved. My religious grandmother would never condone aborting her grandchild. I was sure she would support marriage. We arrived at her house in Camino, sat at the long table in the kitchen, and answered her questions while holding hands. Bill, sitting opposite and off to the side, said nothing; his hearing aid was off. I'm not sure he knew what was going on.

After a short while, even before she served dinner, Grandma motioned me onto the laundry porch next to the concrete washtubs. Brisk and agitated, she clutched my arm. With an insistent whisper she hissed, "You have to give that baby away!"

"Grandma, what are you talking about? This is my baby!" In utter surprise, I turned half away from her, my arm draped across my abdomen.

"You can't raise that child; just think what it will *look* like. You have to give it up for adoption."

I glanced around the corner at my boyfriend, a tall, strong, perfectly proportioned athlete. Ron also had acne, mousy looking hair, and spaces between his teeth. In my view these flaws were temporary, correctable. But despite his ironed madras shirt, hopsack jeans, and suede desert boots, Grandma Bishop judged Ron subpar. She rejected the baby, a child of her own bloodline.

"Grandma Bishop is not feeling well," I murmured to Ron. I placed my hand on his shoulder as I gathered my sweater and pocketbook. "We'd better go so she can rest." We left. I never told him what she said, but I have to admit, on that night to me Ron looked like a big, clueless boy. Protecting the baby was my focus now.

At sixteen and seventeen, we were minors. The only power we had was the power to say no. No adoption. No abortion. I was taken out of school and nothing was said to anyone, not even Debby. My parents viewed the pregnancy as a shameful tragedy. Jiggs banished me from rides in his customized Chevy, the cruelest punishment he could conjure. Mom took me to Dr. Williams. I confronted him for accusing me of plagiarism years before. He remained unruffled, asking, "Well, yes, Elisa, what *about* your writing?"

I dismissed his implication, saying, "I don't need to go to school to write," adding with naïve assurance, "I can write anywhere, anytime."

My little brother Ed, a freshman in high school, spent time inventing things, never studying. Hyper and funny, his dyslexia was severe, and his grades were low, despite Mom's work with him to improve his reading. After my parents' near divorce, Ed maneuvered carefully, staying neutral in our parents' simmering, subterranean conflict by smoking pot most days. Following the confirmation of my pregnancy, he became a kind ally.

"Elisa, do you want me to empty the dishwasher or set the table tonight?" he asked one afternoon. My little brother was maturing. He was the only one who sought to ease the anxiety I felt after setting all of this in motion.

My parents, determined to separate me from Ron, decided to send me to Seattle to work as a nanny for a relative of my high school counselor. I had no choice but to agree to this plan. "No matter where I am, I will never get rid of my baby. I will never get an abortion, and adoption is *out*."

A few days before the trip to Seattle, Mom and I shopped for maternity clothes. The expandable panel on the pants and the loose, feminine tops sparked a private blush of delight in me, a delight I sought to hide. While assisting me in the dressing room, Mom broke down in tears.

"I'm sorry," she said as she dabbed her eyes with a tissue, "but this is not how I expected to be doing this with you."

I started to reach for her but held back, afraid I'd make things even worse.

FIFTEEN

Kenny Kenny Kenny, Seattle, 1966

After a snowy, two-day car ride with my high school counselor, I arrived at the Blumenthals' split-level ranch house on the outskirts of Seattle. Greeting us at the door, the couple smiled and stepped aside, introducing their twelve-year-old son, Randy. Then Kenny, the adopted four-year-old I was to nanny, raced into the room, slid across the hardwood floor, and flopped flat out on the entry rug, kicking his heels into the carpet in a weird horizontal dance. Eyes wild and hands twirling in the air, he ignored his father's yell: "Kenny! Kenny! Kenny!"

At last Kenny lay still, panting, his hair and forehead wet with sweat.

The father, Irv, looked at me and said, "Elisa, this is Kenny; he's excited to meet you."

At dinner that night, Kenny refused to eat, a devilish dare-you expression on his face. Irv gave him one warning, then shoved Kenny's face into the plate, nearly suffocating him. At so-called naptime the next day, they carted him wailing and kicking up the stairs, then pitched him into his room, bolting the door from the outside. He kicked the door and the walls, screaming for an hour until "naptime" was over. When I tried to color with him that afternoon, he scribbled furiously over the page and onto the table in a rage.

It was winter in the Pacific Northwest. The hazy sky and flat landscape seemed blank, unfinished. There was no canyon, no mountain on the horizon, just cloudy rain. The first few days I followed after Kenny, catching him before he tore, kicked, or tossed whatever was in his path. Randy was a nice enough kid; when he was home from school he stayed out of the way of the ruckus.

It fell to me to make Kenny take a nap. What they had been doing was not working, so I decided to try the opposite. Gathering a wriggling Kenny, I held him tight against my chest from shoulders to knees as I slowly walked upstairs, all the while making a random whispering sound. Maybe the sound would calm him like it did the infants I used to babysit. Pressing him onto his bed, more or less pinning him down and whispering the uneven shushing sound, I petted his head with my other hand. He yelled for the first forty minutes and wriggled and resisted in sudden surges most of the hour that first day. When I let him up, we were both drenched in sweat. His nap was over.

By the third day, a minute change had taken place. Kenny nodded in rhythm with the petting, while otherwise pretending to resist. Day by day he improved until on the tenth day, when collected he went instantly limp, pretending to already be asleep. In his room, he sometimes fell asleep while I smoothed his shirt and softly petted his forehead. His parents took Kenny's progress in stride, without comment. I did the housework, ironing, and laundry, and babysat full time while Mrs. Blumenthal spent most days shopping or with her friends.

Irv Blumenthal had a boxed collection of classical music, and there was a record player in my bedroom. Vivaldi, Tchaikovsky, and Rachmaninoff chords and trills helped me create imaginary nature scenes. Each evening, after all my chores were done, I put on a record and made up stories for my baby as we floated together in this soundscape.

Ron's letters usually included a bit of cash from his job at a gas station. After a month I had thirty-seven dollars. But a one-way bus ticket home was over a hundred dollars. Ron said my mother told him not to send me money because I would "just spend it all on a diamond ring." If she really knew me, she would have known I didn't even like diamonds. He continued to send small amounts of money. I wrote to him almost every day.

Kenny progressed. We practiced coloring and building things with blocks (and not knocking them down). He ate his food on his own. As my pregnancy began to show, Irv became irked with me. When I was making a snack one evening, he came into the kitchen.

"We're not getting paid for you to stay here, you know," he said.

Wow. I stopped spreading Miracle Whip on my bologna sandwich. What should I do? Stop eating? I took my sandwich to my room, cloaked in resentment and shame.

One evening a month later, I was sitting in the family room, crocheting an afghan in heather brown and creamy yellow for my future house. Kenny came tearing around the corner and tripped over my feet. As I reached to help him up, Irv yelled, "How dare you trip my son!"

Retreating to my room, playing a record as low as it would go, I lay beneath the covers. I reverted to a cottony dull-witted place, focused on tending to Kenny and housekeeping. I did not feel safe. The baby fluttered about, keeping me company. Meanwhile my breasts and belly bloomed, rounding.

I wrote to Ron and my parents, pleading to come home. Ron

sent the rest of the money for the bus. As I left, Kenny clung to my legs, begging me to stay. I had to pry him away. At the last minute, his parents offered me the entire boxed collection of classical records, but I declined, mostly out of spite. I might not have a good record player for a long time.

The affordable ticket was on a local route and lasted over twenty hours. I kept to myself, listening to my favorite songs, "96 Tears" and "The Letter" on the fancy transistor radio Dad had bought me for my thirteenth birthday, an eternity ago—when the river ran warm; when Tommy was my boyfriend; when I believed I knew the secret of how to be human.

Late at night, Ron came to meet me at the bus station, first grabbing my suitcases, then setting them down and holding me close in a strong hug.

That night in his bedroom at his parent's house, Ron was tentative, curious about the baby. Could he feel it kick?

"Here, try putting your hand here," I told him as a familiar flutter passed across my abdomen, deep inside. Neither of us knew how to be what we had been to each other or even to ourselves, nor what our future would hold. We just knew we had made it this far.

As Ron slept, my mind moved in a fast current, looping between fear and hope. Would we make it, could we build a future? How? At last I slept and dreamt I was giving birth underwater, deep in the river beneath the bridge. In the dream I held my breath and struggled to bring my newborn baby to the surface. But before we broke through, before we were safe, I awoke in the damp rumpled bed, my heart skittering fast.

SIXTEEN

The Unknowable, 1967

Remember my independent study when I was eight: If you think you're happy, are you? I had a new question now. If you think you're strong, are you? Here I was, day one at Ron's.

Laughter and conversation in the dining room mingled with sounds from the kitchen where the percolator was pumping away. From my seat at the table I could see Kate, standing at the stove, give a firm spank to a big hunk of pale pink hamburger, flattening it and dropping it in a frying pan. Cheap hamburger for breakfast?

Lacy eggs sizzled in hamburger grease, a bowl of gray milk gravy, and a pile of white toast traveled by me. Lazy swirls of smoke floated above us in the dim morning light; the butter dish in the center of the table doubled as the family ashtray.

"Um, Kate, I think I'll make myself some oatmeal." I hadn't had morning sickness for months, but with the grease, the smoke, and the gray milk in that gravy boat, nausea threatened.

In the sink I found a dented aluminum pan. On the counter leaned a jumbo box of Tide laundry soap. There was no other soap of any kind in the room. I took a few granules and some super-hot water and cleaned the little pan as best I could. As the oatmeal cooked, the small pot did a little dance. The metal was so thin it could hardly withstand the heat of the burner. All the while a faint whiff of Tide burned off the outside of the pan.

There was no way I could stay here.

As I sat eating my oatmeal, I explained to Ron and his family that I really owed it to my parents to go and see them; in fact, the sooner the better. Two hours later I was back at the river.

My father met me at the door, glanced at my belly, and bolted for the bathroom to vomit. My mother turned away, silently crying. I went to my bedroom, lay down on my twin bed, curled around myself, and stared at the wall.

Within two weeks my parents agreed to let us marry.

At a judge's house outside of Placerville, Mom, Ron, and I filled out a bit of paperwork while Dad stayed in the parking lot. I could hear his constant pacing in the gravel driveway. The judge's wife, dressed in a shaggy chenille bathrobe, was our other witness, and throughout the brief ceremony she leaned against the doorjamb, languidly smoking a cigarette. I stood beside Ron wearing a tent of a blue dress. He wore his gas station uniform; he had to go straight to work when we were done.

As we came out the door, Dad lunged up, taking a swing at Ron as he came down the stairs. Ron was two inches taller and had a powerful reach. He could hammer Dad flat in two seconds. Instead he ducked and shifted as Mom grabbed Dad's arm, saying her ubiquitous, "Joe, no . . ." I barely registered the scuffle. Sheltering my belly, I headed to the car. I was married now. To Ron. Moving, that was the key. On this day, my trademark endurance was worn as thin as the aluminum pans in Kate's kitchen. My only recourse was to stay in motion.

Our first apartment cost forty dollars a month, furnished. Ron walked to his job. We could not afford a car or telephone.

My aunt and uncle gave us a crib for a wedding present. I spent my days cleaning and re-cleaning the two cramped rooms. The filmy nylon curtains that came with the place disintegrated in my hands when I washed them. Still, I believed it was my duty to make a happy home. I set coins aside for my husband's new work shoes. I learned to cook so everything was ready at the same time.

After a few weeks, Dad offered us the old house by the bridge, rent-free. He gave us an old turquoise pick up truck from his used car lot. In exchange we agreed to manage Dad's small trailer park. Ron hauled the tenant's garbage to the dump each week, and I collected the rent and cleaned the restrooms and the laundry room. The rundown house was unchanged, but now the sun porch, my bedroom from long ago, became the nursery. My parents even cosigned on some colonial style furniture I chose from the Sears catalogue. It was cheap and surprisingly comfortable. The style, never my favorite, seemed to suit the knotty pine interior.

On June 30, the day the baby was due, a new electronic sign outside the bank showed the time and temperature: Noon, 104 degrees. I parallel parked the old truck. After depositing the trailer park rent, I decided to swing by Kate's for some iced tea. Jesus, it was hot. Kate had a series of paperbacks, the *Falconhurst* saga. Sex, violence, hundreds of pages of ripped bodices and racial tension set in the pre-Abolition south. I was hooked on this version, a kind of *Gone with the Wind* gone wild.

I fell asleep in her little back bedroom, the book under my cheek. Every ten minutes I woke up. After an hour I realized I was in the early stages of labor, right on time. The baby was due on June 30. Everything was going to be fine.

We lingered at Kate's a few hours until Ron got off work. At the hospital my obstetrician, Dr. Letts (his real name), checked on me; after a couple of hours he said, "Okay, you can start your breathing now."

"I am breathing," I answered.

"I thought you said you were doing natural childbirth; didn't you take classes?"

"What classes? I'm strong. You just do it, like on *Wagon Train*."

In the delivery room, the nurses set up bright lights, strapped me down with my legs open, and then just waited. Minutes ticked by. Where was the doctor? Suddenly I had an overwhelming sense of dread, an intense need to push, to get the baby born.

"Where's the doctor? I have to push. There's something wrong with my baby." I struggled to sit up, but the nurses restrained me, one on each side. "There's something wrong, I'm telling you. I have to have my baby *now*."

Above me a nurse said wearily, "I don't know what it is about these young girls, they do fine for a while, and then . . ."

At last Dr. Letts came in. As soon as I heard the door swing, I started to push, and the baby slipped out. I heard a nurse's sharp intake of breath.

The table started rocking, a small movement, rhythmic.

"What is it?" I asked. I struggled to sit up.

"You have a boy, dear," one nurse said.

"No, I mean, what's wrong, what's wrong with my baby?" I pleaded.

"He's not breathing just yet. You rest. We're taking care of him," the other nurse replied.

I slumped back and, with the heat and the gentle rocking of the table, fell into some kind of sleep. The rocking stopped. The doctor's face floated above me, tears welling in his eyes and into the top edge of his cloth mask. He was shaking his head. "I'm so sorry."

I smelled rubbing alcohol, felt a swab on my upper arm.

"*Wait!* Just let me hold my baby! Let me tell my husband myself. I don't need a shot."

They gave me the shot.

The umbilical cord was uncommonly short and wrapped around the baby's neck. His blood supply and oxygen were cut off while I lay there begging to deliver my child. They say very young mothers have a higher incidence of this short cord deviation. No one said anything about me crying out, warning something was wrong. Not a word was said about my plea to hold my stillborn baby, to tell my husband myself. My strength and resilience, marshaled time and again over sixteen years, was rendered inaccessible by the narcotic administered by the nurses and doctor.

Unconscious for more than ten hours, I never saw the baby, never held him. I was in the deepest reaches of the unknowable. My mother told me later that Ron stood by my bed, refusing to leave the room, but he was powerless to comfort me. That shot, given against my will, robbed me of my chance to process, to rise up, to greet and then release my baby son.

This could not be undone.

AFTER THE FIRE,
SPRING 2018

When the rain stopped, the empty burned lots sprouted spring grasses. Lush mounds of poppies and spiky bright daffodils decorated the dark earth. Because the rain was over, heavy equipment moved in. All the devastation would be scraped deep and carted away, including the bright blossoms and green grass. Then the remaining earth must be tested for carcinogenic remnants and, if needed, scraped even deeper. It's the law. For some fire survivors, this scraping is the deepest cut. No more sifting the ash for a lost diamond, no more collecting fragments of china.

In late March, fifty homeowners on our road formed a neighbors' group dedicated to emergency preparedness. We exchanged stories of the terror, our gratitude that no one died, our relief no one was injured. I volunteered to take CPR, first aid, and AED training and completed the course in three weeks. I carted home a costly AED machine, prepared to revive heart attack and drowning victims. Taking action is in my wheelhouse. When we evacuate now—which has happened twice since 2017—I take the medical kit and the AED with me. When we travel, I hand it off to a neighbor at the bottom of the road.

In the San Francisco studio one afternoon as we waited for samples of *chinoiserie* to dry, my son James tried to explain away my remorse about not alerting neighbors the night of the fire.

"That night? Mom, you and Chuck had no way to know there was another fire burning half a mile away. Probably lots of people ran," James said as he stirred some cream into his coffee. "Maybe rushing down the mountain in the middle of the night was just instinct."

"But that's not the point. What if someone *had* died?"

As a young girl I'd been a lifeguard, a scout, and had assisted my mother with emergencies. I was at the ready to help, at least in my mind. Running away was the last thing I expected of myself. Yet my connection with any lizard, any tender fern, seemed much more alive than my connection to random neighbors. The night of the fire seemed to prove that.

Years of scanning buildings for flaws and imbalances worked for my career, but the scanning did not stop there. I often scanned people, strangers and acquaintances, and offered glib advice, later learning I had been insensitive. My communication style is abrupt, more like my father and grandmother than I like to admit. What would it take to fix this?

It was time to do some of my own deep scraping. I wanted to bulldoze, to excavate down to bedrock, to find my own human kindness, forgiveness, and trust.

SEVENTEEN

Alchemy, 1967

When I was discharged from the hospital, my parents took me to their house for a few days. Ron could come too, a huge concession. While I was still at the hospital, my mother packed up the baby's nursery and took everything to the storeroom in their garage.

I realize now my mother showed love by tending us from a distance. She ironed our shoelaces. Cut the crust off our sandwiches. Put a note in our lunch boxes on Valentine's Day. Moved the nursery to spare me the pain. This distance was familiar—so familiar I often overlooked any message it contained. I vowed there would be no distance between my own child and me. I planned to bring my baby everywhere; we would laugh, we would sing, we would be together. My secret hope? I could heal my own aloneness along the way.

Now what?

Jiggs was away at college, so Ron and I stayed in his room. From my brother's double bed, I had a view out the sliding glass door to the north side of the canyon and the Tarzan vines across the river. I could hear the tamed, regulated water running low and slow outside. I lay there, adrift. I found myself thinking about offers my parents had made when I first got pregnant.

"You can go to any college you want; you can spend a year in Europe. Don't throw your life away."

Tremendous emptiness echoed all around. Just three days after the baby failed to live, I lay there weighing my options, contemplating leaving, moving far, far away, even Europe. Without the baby, spending my life with Ron seemed limited, small. Over the past few months I began to suspect that Ron was not . . . very smart. Certainly, he lacked vision. But should he be faulted for this? He was kind, he was earnest, and he was now as adrift as I was. Could I divorce him at a time like this?

Just then my father gave a one-tap knock on the half open door and entered the room. I hadn't seen him since the baby's stillbirth. "Well, daughter, what are you going to do now? Get a divorce?" He looked down at me, his face angry and dark.

I struggled to sit up, mostly to buy some time. *My God, this is the first thing he says to me after I lose a child?* Then I heard myself speak my lines, straight from some cheesy soap opera. "How can you ask that? You know I love my husband. I would never leave him." Even as I said this, I heard one of Dad's favorite sayings in my head: *"You're digging your own grave."*

Dad recited a litany of complaints against my grieving eighteen-year-old husband. Ron didn't thank my mother for lunch; he just took the lunch bag and went to work. Ron said almost nothing at dinner. Ron was ungrateful, a caveman. I waved Dad out of the room, layered more covers over myself and huddled down, cold to the bone.

When I was philosophizing about being sensitive—the positive kind—way back when I was twelve, I believed a promise was sacred. I promised Ron getting pregnant was a good idea. I promised I would marry him. Just now I vowed to never leave him. But these promises seemed minor compared to the private vow I'd failed to keep.

"I will keep you safe," I had promised the baby every single day.

I should have cried out louder in the delivery room, pushed the baby into the world no matter what the nurses said. This loss would echo through my life. This loss was mine to bear, and it could not be undone.

I see now that my father had insight, and it caused him pain to see me suffer. But he could not know the deeper cause of my pregnancy. I couldn't explain, did not even recognize how the loss of pride after Notre Dame, loss of hope after Tommy, and ultimately the loss of the river and all it represented opened a chasm of grief that making a baby promised to fill. And all these losses were compounded by the secret shame inflicted by my grandparents so very long ago.

Months passed before I asked Mom if she had seen the baby. She described him clinically, noting he was "long limbed and looked like a normal baby." This didn't give much solace. Decades passed before I asked if she held him.

"Um, yes, Elisa," she said. "I didn't tell you because I was afraid it would upset you." More distance. Now, so many years later, I think I have cracked the code. She was protecting me, though at the time only the distance registered.

Ron and I returned to the old house by the bridge, and in eight weeks I lost almost thirty pounds. I kept telling people I was okay until I started fainting. My mother insisted I visit the local psychiatrist, Dr. Shipley. Entering his office, my heart sank. The doctor was tremendously fat; he filled the whole space behind his broad desk. How could such an unhealthy man help me get well?

I explained losing the baby and mentioned the fainting. Dr.

Shipley nodded, saying this was caused by anxiety. He took his notepad and began to write a prescription. Pills?

"I don't need pills. I need to feel my feelings, not *dull* them," I said, leaving the prescription on his desk.

Once home, I strode into the kitchen where the walls were paneled with thick planks of knotty pine. In one swift motion, I swung a sturdy kitchen chair over my head and beat it again and again and again at the wall, the floor, back at the wall, bellowing out, "*No! No! No! No! No!*" Slumping to the floor, sweaty and panting, I curled on my side and whispered, "I'm sorry, I'm sorry," to my faraway baby.

The kitchen rampage calmed me, but something heavy lingered, a thick sediment of fear. Did the baby die because I loved him too much? Could I have loved him to death? Catholicism held no clues, and the grasshoppers, the rattlesnakes, and the piles of rock beside the river stayed silent on the matter. When in doubt, when in fear, I knew one solution—keep moving.

I began to act as if I were fine. I took care of the trailer park. I made sensible, affordable meals for Ron using recipes cut out from *Family Circle* magazine. We adopted two stray kittens. I decorated our Christmas tree with white birds and no tinsel, not one strand.

I never went into the empty sunroom.

In the pantry one afternoon, still wearing my bathrobe while deciding between instant vanilla pudding or instant chocolate pudding for my hard-working husband's dessert, I looked around as though for the first time. Suddenly my setting and my choices seemed ridiculous. *Look at me, safe and free. Free to choose which cheap pudding to make for a boy who was my husband.* And sure, I was safe—deep in a canyon, inside a ramshackle house, going nowhere.

Ron returned home each night grimy and hungry, smelling of gas and oil. Sad himself, he orbited around me, watchful, wondering what we were to do. Meanwhile, I negotiated the margins of our marriage as I cleaned and cooked and pretended not to be sad. All the while I held myself in an emotional half turn, like my mother appeared in those family pictures long ago.

I was the woman crying at the kitchen window now.

What alchemy could transform this sadness? Submerged in feelings of shame, with no access to the sun, I felt like a golem of a girl masquerading as a woman. My little girl promises—to be caring and sensitive—fluttered like tattered prayer flags while all around rang the big, tolling bells of aloneness and loss.

A small glimmer, a mystical message came to me that winter in my dreams. For weeks, each night as I descended into sleep, pages of unknown ancient writing appeared, revealing the secret of life on Earth. Comprehending and agreeing completely with each sentence, in the dream I felt drenched through and through with golden joy. But each morning, as I awakened, this writing and its meaning melted away. I could not conjure the essence of the words and had no reference for the lettering. Yet I felt strengthened and somewhat reassured.

EIGHTEEN

Out of the Echoing Emptiness, 1967–1968

t was time to move away from the river, out of the canyon before another winter closed in. What friends we had were gone to college or Vietnam or working jobs in other places. Our world was small and shrinking. For now, Ron was exempt from the draft because we were married. If we had a baby, this exemption would be more absolute. Every month I looked for signs I was pregnant. No luck, not even monthly periods. I released no eggs.

I was no longer viable.

We moved uptown to a sunny cottage surrounded by tall pines. Warm golden planks lined the living room walls, and a black potbellied woodstove stood in one corner. It was cold, and, returning home after another disappointing appointment with my new gynecologist, Dr. Bliss (his real name), I stoked up a woodblock fire. Wrapped in the brown-and-yellow afghan, I pulled the cushy Sears rocker near the woodstove.

"Okay, God. This is it. I'm sitting here by the fire until I hear from you. Will I have a healthy baby *this year* or should I turn my energy to something else? I can't go on with this waiting. If I'm definitely *not* going to have a baby this year, tell me, and I'll find a new direction. If I *am* going to have a baby, I need to know before I leave this chair."

I sat and rocked and stoked the fire. After forty-five minutes, as the woodblocks slumped and shrunk, things looked grim. No word. No sign. No sign is not "a sign." I stopped rocking and closed my eyes. Listening to the embers fall and the pines whisper in the breeze outside, I fell asleep. When I woke moments later, I felt renewed. Then, at that moment, I felt the fountain of light, the same fountain of life I felt with the first pregnancy. I laughed out loud, clapped, and leapt to my feet. We were going to have a baby.

Ron and I told no one, of course. Who would believe I conjured a child by sitting beside a potbellied stove? But I believed, and though Ron did not absolutely confirm he believed, he did not reject the idea, saying, "I remember last time, and you turned out to be right then." I took this as a ringing endorsement.

On Monday morning I went back to Dr. Bliss, requesting another lab test. The receptionist, the nurse and the doctor told me it was pointless. I had just been examined a few days before and there was no sign of pregnancy.

"Just please do the lab test, I'll wait here for the results," I said, seating myself in the waiting room.

It took a couple hours for the lab to report. Then, in the examination room, after pressing and prodding, Dr. Bliss confirmed that I was six weeks pregnant. "The baby will come at the end of October."

"I know it looks to you like it's due then, but I just got pregnant on Friday. This baby is really going to be born in early December," I told him.

The day the pregnancy test came back positive was also the day in 1968 when the exemption for men with one child was lifted. Fathers and fathers-to-be would no longer escape the draft; they would train and be shipped posthaste to Vietnam. Within a month Ron had his orders, and in the six weeks before he left, he slowly faded before my eyes, losing confidence and faith in our future, his future, anything. We talked about hiding out in Canada, somehow escaping the draft. We petitioned the draft board to no avail. Ron just faded away, and then he was gone.

My design for our family was unrealistic now. The wood paneled, sunny place up on the ridge was too expensive for me on Ron's army pay. I moved home to my parents but said nothing about the pregnancy. I planned to go to business school in Sacramento.

First, the admissions officer explained, since I'd never graduated from high school I had to take an aptitude test. When I returned the completed forms she looked surprised. "Take your time, dear, check your answers carefully," she said. I'd already checked them twice. While my test was graded, I scanned the course catalog for a program I could finish before the baby's due date. The best was an all day, every day, nine-month computer course.

"You should be very proud," crooned the admissions counselor. "You scored higher than the average *male* college graduate!" I arranged to challenge the writing and spelling courses to shorten the program and applied for a scholarship. I graduated with an A+ rating four months early. Done.

Meanwhile, at each checkup, Dr. Bliss worried the baby was underdeveloped, underweight. Every couple of months I reminded him the due date was six weeks later than he calculated. When I was six months along, I finally told my parents. My mom cried, not from happiness. Dad didn't throw up this time. He just walked away, shaking his head.

I found a two-room apartment in Placerville behind a rambling shingle house. Dad helped me paint the bathroom and kitchen cabinets, saying, "Elisa, you are never going to finish painting at this rate. Watch me now, dip the brush, tap it twice, then spread the paint, using even pressure. *You* control the paint; don't let the paint control you." Years later I used this lesson with new apprentices. When it came to physical labor, Dad knew what he was talking about.

We moved my Sears furniture, the rug, the bed and dresser, and the sturdy table and chairs. With delight I watched the sunlight spread across my little living room all through the day, creating patterns made by branches of a giant oak outside. My French door opened to a broad slate patio under the massive tree. This sheltered, solitary place felt innocent and safe. I was happy.

Ron, a trained infantryman, came home briefly before he was dispatched to Fort Polk, Louisiana, to learn more killing techniques. Vietnam was an absolute in his future. The army had him in fighting shape, but his heart was not in it. He was shaky, trembled, and hardly spoke. When we learned his best friend had been killed in Vietnam, my husband shut down completely. Yet he had to go. It was the law, so he left for Louisiana.

After some thought, I phoned a young man named Blaine who babysat for my family while he was in high school. He lived in San Francisco now and was rumored to be a Communist. Maybe Blaine knew a way to get Ron out of the army.

I left a cryptic message with one of Blaine's roommates. A few days later he called back to say we were on. In 1968, I was eighteen and drove to San Francisco for the first time on my own. After two hours of missed turns and bypassed streets, I finally arrived. Blaine looked sharper than I remembered, more defined, somehow hip. His apartment was spare, and everything seemed foreign. He used a glass beaker and poured boiling water over special paper filters to make coffee. We drank it out of tiny cups. Wow.

Patient and focused, Blaine already had a plan. For the next two hours he shared his strategy involving pro-bono lawyers, safe houses, and timelines. I had some chores, mostly proving Ron was needed more at home than overseas. We planned to go the safest route, a hardship discharge. There were no guarantees; deserters could go to prison for twenty years. Ron would have to go AWOL after his final round of training and turn himself in at the Presidio in San Francisco when the time was right. Trial prep could take months.

We met up again when Ron, now just barely twenty years old, was home on a short leave. He was subdued, uncertain, but agreed to go AWOL. This plan became our organizing principle, with feelings taking a back seat.

Throughout the second pregnancy I was careful. Careful not to over-bond. Not to smother. Not to kill. Privately I hoped for a boy. I was unsure if I could teach a girl how to be a woman. I was not a natural homemaker like Aunt Betty. And my mother? Mostly she wanted me to calm down, sit still, and read. Being good at being a woman remained a mystery. Better to have a boy.

NINETEEN

Hallelujah Chorus, 1968

n 1968, Grandma Bishop had a serious stroke. From then on she was paralyzed on one side. Her driving days were over. No more legendary potato soup. No more volunteer work. No more canning pears and whole blackberries and storing them in perfect rows on shelves in her cool dirt basement.

Her sudden frailty was a tremendous shock to her. The moment she got home from the hospital, she started complaining and couldn't seem to stop. She never used to complain, not ever. She railed at her husband, ridiculing him over and over for little things like buying the wrong lettuce seeds. Bill was not exactly with it, and he might have bought the wrong seeds whether she had a stroke or not. He was pretty feeble. Anyhow, he crumpled. He paced around the house muttering as Grandma lay in her bed, directing his every action. When I arrived at the house soon after she came home from the hospital, she wailed, "Elisa, he won't clean like I tell him, he refuses to even wax the floor! He says I might slip—he says I will fall."

I buffed her appliances with Jubilee kitchen polish but left the floor unwaxed.

She had been home a couple of months when, late one after-noon, my father got a call. "You'd better come up here, Joe," she said. "Bill took off his hearing aids, his glasses, and left his watch and his wallet on the table. He walked out the door with his shotgun."

With her new garbled speech, it took Dad a minute to deci-pher what Grandma Bishop was saying. He called the sheriff then hightailed it up to Camino. For the next three days Dad and the police searched for a sign of Bill Bishop day and night, but even the tracking dogs found nothing.

Many months later at a family dinner, my father held high his cocktail, tinkling the ice, and announced loudly, "Old Bill, he knew what he was doing. Just walk away. That's the way to do it. He told me a long time ago, 'Joe, if I ever get sickly I'll just put an end to it. I got a spot all picked out.'" After a pause and another sip of bourbon Dad continued. "I found him. I saw him, and I said, well, what the hell, leave him there, that's what he wanted."

When we pressed for more details, Dad said, "No, that's it. I promised him I wouldn't tell anybody and, by God, I'm not tell-ing you now." We couldn't be sure Dad was telling the truth; he was known to exaggerate, especially when he was drinking.

For years when driving at dusk, I sometimes thought I saw Bill Bishop in his work hat and overalls, beside the road up ahead, slowly walking away.

Not long after he disappeared, Grandma Bishop was moved to a convalescent home. Her children had taken control. The two-story schoolhouse, her furniture, her car, all sold off. Aunt Betty asked me to come to Grandma's and choose "nice things for entertaining." Pressed glass luncheon plates? Silver salt cellars and crystal olive dishes for me to use in my tiny apartment? No thanks.

After completing his training, Ron went AWOL as planned, hiding out in San Francisco with Blaine's comrades in a condemned apartment building. Ron never worked during those months. He claimed it was too dangerous because he couldn't use his social security number. Now he was just a nothing, doing nothing, guilty of desertion.

He couldn't come around Placerville. The draft board, made up of Dad's friends from Rotary, would turn Ron in if they saw him in town. We decided he should stay away; I could have the baby by myself. It was the second time, after all.

In early December Dr. Bliss insisted on inducing. By my calculations, the baby was just about due, so I agreed. I brought along my crocheting, a variegated blue, pink, and cream baby blanket, and planned to finish the border during labor.

The nurse started the Pitocin drip, and I crocheted, my eye on the big wall clock. Once in a while, I would take a long breath and reassure the baby. Never a full, deep breath, I held back out of habit, cautious to the bone.

When a nurse came to check on me I waved her away, saying, "This is my second baby. I'm fine." I made it halfway around the border when I experienced tremendous pain. Not even an hour had passed, but suddenly the contractions were twenty seconds apart and lasting two minutes. Something was not right.

I rang the nurse.

"Oh! You're ready to deliver. We have to move you," she said. The unfinished blanket slipped to the side and trailed along behind us as I was wheeled down the hall.

In the delivery room, there was a sharp pain when they broke my water. It was time to push.

Almost immediately I heard a rasping sound, like a cat's dry meowing, and out slipped my baby, a red, wrinkly boy. An immense chorus of heavenly voices filled the air, a thousand angels, each singing one long true note, created a harmonic tapestry of sound, filling all the space around us. I began to laugh and cry, then cry and laugh. I was so relieved, so, so relieved. Hallelujah!

I held him close until the nurse took him to the nursery. Back in my room, an aide put a bowl beneath me and showed me how to knead my stomach to stop the bleeding. Blood splashed into the bowl, so much that it splashed onto her shoes. She left, returning with a bigger bowl and a blood pressure cuff. I seemed to be bleeding a lot.

Then another bowl, and a different cuff.

"I can't get a reading," she said as she stripped the second cuff off my arm. "This one seems to be broken too. I'll be right back." Her voice sounded weak and distant. I rubbed and rubbed my loose fluffy belly as instructed, feeling faint, then fainter. When she returned I saw ten of her, ten of everything. Blood was everywhere. I called for my mother, my father. Another cuff was wrapped on my arm.

"It's not broken, can't you see? I'm bleeding out. Get my parents, I want to say goodbye."

Again the chorus of a thousand angels filled the room. I began to melt into the rich vibration of color and sounds, into essence, disintegrating as a person and integrating molecule by molecule into an immense unbounded energy.

Some hours later, the sound of muffled moaning brought me around. I heard someone say, "I don't love my husband. I don't love my husband. Just let me go. I want to be with my baby." I thought I had just had my first baby, stillborn . . . It took some time for the nurse to convince me I had a healthy boy.

I was drenched in incandescent joy when I held Jamey, my new son. Everything was hyper real; each item in the room seemed super defined, purposeful, radiating a message. All was absolute; all was profound. I cradled my baby and began to sing improvised lullabies.

When the nurses tried to return Jamey to the nursery, I held him fiercely to my chest. I made up a poem and put it to song. When they brought my crocheting, I let them take the baby so I could finish my work. When at last I quieted down, I heard the haunting echo of that moaning woman.

"I don't love my husband. I don't love my husband."

I wrapped the wool through my fingers, hooking and pulling, weaving the border loop by loop, finishing the edge all in cream.

For weeks I was marked. Pin dots of capillary blood showed at every pore over my face, neck, and arms. Huge bruises covered my arms from the elbow down. Amniotic fluid had entered my bloodstream, causing a bleeding disorder. If the labor had taken even moments longer, Jamey would have died. The odds of survival for mother and child with this condition were one in eight hundred. The disorder was rare, one in 80,000 births, and small hospitals had little experience dealing with it. My mother, a former obstetrics nurse, recognized the symptoms and alerted the staff. After multiple blood transfusions and special blood products, hepatitis was a near certainty for both Jamey and me. But I wasn't worried. I was alive, and so was my son.

TWENTY

Together Forever, 1969

My perception of life had been changed by the angel song, the delirium of death wrapped around the raw vibrancy of life. When I tried to explain this experience, I sounded crazy.

"Everything is vibration. Color and sound all blend when you die; you just melt into it. Everything you hear and see here is a representation of this vibration, an agreement of molecules, and, uh . . ." I gave up trying to explain, even to myself. I had plenty to do caring for Jamey.

The cozy apartment under the giant shade tree became our retreat. Still somewhat disassembled and patched together, I felt vulnerable, uncoordinated, and cumbersome. I refused my mother's help and even put off visits from Ron's mother, Kate. I was not prepared to handle a newborn and didn't want any witnesses. After all my efforts to become a mother, I floundered to find my footing.

Jamey cried and cried; he was quiet only when floating in the sink. With my hand under his head, he languished in the tepid water, calm, peaceful, asleep. Suggestions from Dr. Spock's book on child care, like wrapping him tight or letting him cry, outraged him. Singing, whispering, and rocking, my magic formula for Kenny, worked for half an hour or forty-five minutes, and then Jamey would break into full cries, arms thrown wide, arching his back and screeching like an enraged pterodactyl. We were in alien territory, both of us.

Afternoons those first two weeks (when baby books suggest new mothers take a nap while their newborns slept) were no different from morning or the dead of night. Forty-five minutes of sleep, twenty minutes of Jamey crying, ten minutes floating him in the sink, maybe another round of sleeping. When he was a few days old, his umbilical cord was supposed to fall off. It didn't. After his floating session in the sink, I saw the chunky black stub dangling by a thread. It looked painful and inflamed. Wrapping him in a blanket without even a diaper, I ran to the only woman who might be home in the early afternoon, an 80-year-old unmarried lady who lived across the street. I banged on her door in tears, and when she answered, I opened the blanket and asked, "What am I supposed to do?"

She sent me straight away from her doorstep, calling out after me, "Why did you come here? I have no children!" By the time I got home, I realized I was losing it, hauling my infant off to an old woman because I was afraid of making a mistake.

Preparing for motherhood? My plan was to do the opposite of what my parents did. Cuddling, reassuring, playing—I would do all this. My baby would be my partner. I had babysat for years. Babies liked me, even difficult kids like Kenny. Now I could not escape the truth. My son had an agenda of his own, and without an interpreter, I'd have to rely on trial and error. For the next eighteen years.

The two-room apartment was littered with half-folded laundry, crumpled receiving blankets. A big bottle of Hexol, recommended by Grandma Bishop to soothe my stitches, rested on the back of the toilet. My nightgowns soaked down the front with milk every night and every morning. No matter how much I nursed, the milk just flowed whenever Jamey cried. And he cried a lot. Better to have no one over.

Three weeks later, an ad caught my attention in the local paper. Placerville's first computer center would process bank operations for eight branches. Trained data entry people were needed. I got hired for swing shift. Kate agreed to watch Jamey at her place about two miles away. At work I entered data, check by check, making sure each branch was balanced each weeknight. The new giant computers encompassed an entire floor of a three-story building. When the room got too hot, the machines automatically shut down, so sometimes we worked from four in the afternoon to four the next morning, sleeping on the floor for an hour or two while we waited for the machines to cool.

In the beginning, I tried nursing Jamey on my evening break. He wasn't really on a schedule, and neither were the computers. I switched him to formula. When I picked him up from Kate's, his blankets and his little head smelled like Tareytons. Back at my apartment, I tried to rest during the day until it was time for work in the late afternoon.

I began to ache all over and was bone tired but assumed this was due to stress from the job and the dull fear that I was an inadequate mother. I looked haggard and weird. When I went to Dr. Bliss for my checkup, the receptionist took one look at me and called the doctor to the front. He hustled me into an exam room, saying, "You are jaundiced, you have hepatitis, and you might be contagious. You have to be isolated, on complete bed rest. The baby can't be exposed. You'll have to make arrangements for him."

I was hospitalized for several weeks. From time to time, Kate or my mom held Jamey to the window outside my room, making him wave his pudgy fist in my direction. He was healthy, and his tests were good. My tests were not. I was told to lie still; rest was the only cure. I slept and slept.

The longer I stayed there, the more alien I felt. Ron would call from payphones in San Francisco, still dodging the army MPs. We had no way of knowing if they were looking for him.

"How is Jamey doing?" he asked every time. He chose that name, the only connection he had to the baby so far, but to be fair, Ron had to stay away. We were both living in suspended animation.

"He looks okay, but I only see him when they hold him up to the window," I reminded him. "Call your mom; she'll tell you all about it." With little else to say, I felt relieved when, after a quick "Love you," he hung up.

After a month in isolation, when I was discharged from the hospital, Mom took me home to her house. My parents had moved everything out of the apartment while I was recovering, so now my old room was also Jamey's nursery. For the next couple of months I was to rest, sequestered under Mom's care. Purgatory.

Four days later, while Mom was at the store, I packed up Jamey and all I imagined we'd need and drove to San Francisco. On the 140-mile drive, I pulled off the freeway twice and slept in the car, Jamey beside me. Ron was in the stockade at the Presidio now, as directed by his lawyer. In 1968, so many AWOL soldiers turned themselves in at the Presidio that detainees were *encouraged* to leave after four thirty every afternoon so others could use their bunks. Ron had to check back in at five every morning.

"The sergeant says he's going to watch *Lassie*, and that's code that he won't report anyone who leaves. If there's empty bunks, other guys can sleep there," Ron explained. The "brig" at this time was just an orange armband; those wearing it were prohibited from using the bowling alley and not allowed to buy candy at the base commissary. I picked up Ron each afternoon and returned him in the predawn. In the evenings we worked on his case, assembling letters and double-checking data.

We stayed with Blaine, and when Jamey was seven months old, Ron's court martial proceeding took place. I testified, still somewhat jaundiced, and after hearing about the death of the first baby and the difficulty of Jamey's birth, the court martial board seemed subdued.

"I sent a letter to my husband when he was at Fort Polk," I said, holding up the letter. "It was returned, and written on the envelope was, 'No such serial number, no such person.' For the army, my husband may be nonexistent. But for me he is everything."

When I took my seat, I saw tears in some of the board members' eyes. Despite Ron's desertion and refusal to go to Vietnam, he was fined just one dollar and granted a hardship discharge, a watershed victory thanks to the hard work of Blaine, Ron, and the pro bono lawyer. We were free.

We returned to Placerville. It never occurred to us to go someplace else.

Once Ron found work, sorting rocks at a gravel pit, I decided we should buy a house.

"How can we buy a house? We don't have that kind of money," Ron said.

"Exactly! There's a loan for poor people, right? FHA. We're poor, so we qualify. If I find the house and set up the loan, will you do it?"

"Sure, I guess," he said. Mr. Reluctance.

Before Jamey was a year old, we moved into our new house, a thin-walled, low-roofed, two-bedroom place on a scraggly lot above town. When Ron got home, dusty from rock sorting all day, instead of clearing the yard and planting grass, he just slept on our worn Sears couch. Sullen and defeated, he started talking about quitting his job.

"Look, there's no point in me working. No matter how much money we have, you'll never be satisfied," he said one Sunday afternoon after a day of football and beer with his old high school friends. He wasn't joking, not that he'd given his theory much of a test. The gravel pit was not a gold mine. Ever since his best friend was killed in Vietnam a year earlier, Ron seemed hounded by nagging guilt, as though his avoidance of war contributed to his friend's death. In our little town, a number of draftees had been injured or killed, and the war showed no sign of ending.

The disenchantment spreading over both of us seemed to coincide with buying the house. When we signed the loan and I saw the words "thirty years" on the paperwork, I felt oppressed and sullen myself. Thirty years! Sure, I had agreed to be married forever, but thirty years was way too long to stay married to Ron.

Within three months I filed for divorce. Ron, reluctant to pay child support, showed up only a few times a year, and rarely at the time and place arranged. I was a divorced single mother by the time I turned nineteen.

TWENTY-ONE

Making it Work, 1969-1970

Working three days a week for my father, I eventually earned enough money to rent a small apartment in a brick building above town. At a small day-care place, Jamey played all day with five preschool kids on a square of bright grass inside a white picket fence, eating lunch and taking naps on a consistent schedule.

At Dad's dealership, sequestered in the bookkeeping office, I craved approval. I was sleeping with one of the car salesmen, off and on, and also had a boyfriend near the college. Sex, in the early 1970s, was said to be free and supposedly fun, but to me it was more like a power game.

The entire country was in transition. Desegregation, feminism, abortion rights, and the war in Vietnam polarized families and communities. In Placerville, my parents' unhappy marriage was unraveling in a most public manner. For two years Dad had been having an affair with Marsha, a much younger, very curvy blonde with two young children. Mom, busy completing her master's degree, had been blindsided and humiliated. Many people in town knew of the affair long before she did.

Dad moved to a bachelor pad ideal for a single, Dean Martin type guy—shag carpet, a fancy stereo, spare Danish furniture, stylish bar, the whole bit. The one evening I visited, I was keenly aware of my father's diminished self assuredness. He looked fresh peeled, unprotected as he skimmed about in his socks—so he wouldn't have to vacuum, he said—pointing out modern features of the place, as if showing me that he was fine would shore up his own confidence. He made no mention of Marsha or my mother. We played a short chess game, and I was thankful that Frank Sinatra provided background. We seemed to have so little to say.

On a rainy Saturday afternoon, Mom dropped by my apartment unannounced. She was over fifty, and I was surprised by her visit, but even more by her dewy look. Her voice soft, she said, "This is my birthstone. He remembered." She held a large ruby ring up in the weak light of the cloudy day. "He surprised me with this last night, and we leave for Hawaii on Saturday. He says he has a lot to think about but . . . it seems like we might work this out." My mother was infused with tentative tenderness.

While Dad appeared to court my mother, buying that simulated ruby ring and taking her to Hawaii, his accountants were preparing documents to edge Mom out of as much of the business as possible, relegating her share to a small cash payment and the house on the river. Upon returning from Hawaii, he filed for divorce. Shell-shocked, my mother remained in the lonely four-bedroom house on the river with my younger brother Ed, now a junior in high school, for company. She had been sad before, lonely and disappointed. But now she was *abandoned*, lonely, sad, and disappointed. It took her a year to come to terms with her situation and get the house on the market. By then, Dad and his girlfriend Marsha were married.

When Ed started college, Mom moved to a condo in Sacramento and started working again as a nurse. Jamey and I were invited to live with her if I would promise to complete a two-year program at the community college. I applied for a Pell Grant, welfare, and work/study. I petitioned for a double class load, taking twenty-four units a semester to complete a degree in library science in one year instead of two. I worked evenings until ten cooking at a vegetarian restaurant, and during the two semesters we lived with Mom, I started taking speed: tiny white cross-topped pills I got from Ed's roommate.

All through the early '70s, the feminist movement percolated. At twenty-one I declared myself liberated and went braless, then quit shaving my legs and underarms. One day as we washed dishes together in the kitchen, I reached above Mom to put some plates in the cabinet.

She dropped the pan she was drying, crying out, "Elisa, you have hair under your arms!"

I replied, "Well, yeah, Mom, everyone does, you know."

"You will *not* go in the pool at this apartment complex looking like *that*," she retorted.

For a week I held out, but the dark birds' nests of my underarms and swarthy leg hair did not convey the downy, feminist authenticity I'd envisioned. I shaved.

When we had been living together a couple of months, my mother met a friendly electrical engineer at a singles mixer for middle-aged people. Jack was the opposite of my father: not brash, not crude, not critical. He was pleasant. To me he was predictable and boring.

During the year at community college I had an overlapping string of boyfriends or, more accurately, brief assignations. I made them promise to walk away whenever I said we were "done." No hanging on, no whining. I cycled through more than a dozen guys in those months at Mom's condo, meeting up elsewhere whenever convenient. I kept a list of names with hash marks beside common ones like Bob. I slept with four Bobs.

In those months, I saw Jamey about an hour each day during the week. Being busy meant being unavailable, but without any source of intimacy, I felt completely disconnected. By the time I graduated with honors, I was burned out. Grieving for connection with my son and determined to reunite with some kind of natural rhythm, I decided to change course. I would be healthy, drug-free, and celibate for a year, exchanging speed and meaningless sex for motherhood, chanting, and meditating. Jamey and I moved to a kind of ashram on the outskirts of Sacramento where our bits of furniture and hippie essentials—a food mill, incense, the *I Ching*—fit snugly in a converted chicken coop behind the main house. There were four other children under four years old and two more came weekdays for daycare. None of the adults were close friends, but the chance for Jamey to live with other kids his age seemed like a great option.

Jamey and I settled in. From early morning until one in the afternoon, the parents of the other kids disappeared up the hill to meditate and do yoga. In exchange for rent, I cared for six young boys under the age of five, plus Jamey. Then, from two in the afternoon until closing, I cooked in a vegetarian restaurant.

On sunny mornings I took the kids, a picnic lunch, towels, and two bed sheets to a man-made lake so the tawny, long-haired boys could putter around, paddling in the shallow water. We'd eat lunch sitting on a big sheet spread over the silty sand. Later, while they drowsed, I covered them with the second sheet to shield them from sun and bugs. For half an hour I was free to swim and float in the murky water. When the sheet started doing a Jiffy Pop dance, I returned to shore.

Life slowed down. Chanting and laughing and sitting on a muddy shore with a pile of children smoothed the jagged edges caused by my hyper-focus on school, when I'd used busyness and drugs as a temporary North Star. I began to feel connected, to reclaim joy in simple things like the waving grasses on the hill, the golden highlights in Jamey's hair, and the strumming sound of crickets outside our screened-in chicken coop each evening as the temperature dropped. We were safe, and we were free. My plan was working.

Almost immediately after we moved, my mother and Jack got married. Pleasant conversation was Jack's specialty, within a predictable range of topics: flying his small private airplane, his kind and predictable mother, or minor anecdotes from his government job. His stories were tepid, so I only half-listened. After dinner one night at their place, I stirred a cup of acrid microwave coffee as Jack started a new topic. "Elisa, I never knew much about Placerville until I met your mother. The only time I heard of the place was a long time ago, because my brother had an accident there."

"Really. What kind of accident?" I asked, if only to be polite.

"He worked in heavy construction for a company out of Sacramento. When he was in Placerville putting in a sidewalk, a slab of concrete fell off the crane and crushed his leg. Some kids were playing up on the bank above the site. He was trying to get them out of there when the slab hit him."

"But Jack! Wait! Was this in 1953?"

"That'd be about right."

"Jack, we were those kids ... I snuck out of the house with Jiggs, up to the worksite, and saw a man crushed! When I heard the sirens I thought the police were coming to take me away. I thought all this time he was dead, and it might be my fault."

"No, no, a broken leg. He healed up fine. He said the strap broke; he just happened to be looking up the hill. It was an accident."

And in that instant, twenty-plus years of weighty, secret shame melted away. One less murder. My dead man was alive.

AFTER THE FIRE, SUMMER 2018

Six months after the fire, my father died at ninety-two. Just days earlier I visited Dad and Marsha at their home beside a small lake. Dad sat up in a hospital bed near the window with a view of the water. When he looked my way, I gave him a smile and a thumbs-up. He signaled back to me, raising a thumb, which surprised me because his Alzheimer's was so advanced.

I put my hand on his shoulder, and we communed, or so it seemed. He was shrunken like a baby bird. The raised outline of his sternum was prominent; for the first time, he appeared fragile. Just before leaving, I held his hand and said, "Here's what I know, Dad. I love you and you love me." We thumbs-upped together.

Marsha called me at the hotel where Chuck and I were staying in Vancouver, two days later. When I learned of Dad's death, I felt surprisingly light, not heavy. In a flash the judgment that had followed me like an eye in the sky for my whole life dissolved. While Chuck was in an all-day business meeting, I set out alone on a rigorous hike up a Canadian mountain to consider the presence and absence of my father and my relationship with myself now that he was gone.

Trudging along, I realized I had long weighed my own strengths and weaknesses against what I knew of his and of my grandmother's. We three shared an ingrained tenacity, for that I remain grateful. But the scathing, judgmental appraisal of others? That concerned me. There were times I was as blunt, brisk, and absolute as my grandmother when she scrubbed me, as my father when he criticized my choices as a girl, as a woman. Was this some kind of fossilized pattern, imprinted in childhood, something inescapable?

What then was this delightful airiness, this feeling of freedom? Could it possibly last? As I hiked the steep trail, I realized that claiming and reclaiming my freedom in the coming years was entirely up to me. Just me.

I scanned the trail for a heart-shaped rock, a token from this day. For two decades I had collected like this, and within four steps I found the very stone I sought, smaller than the palm of Dad's hand. The smooth rock warmed as I carried it to the summit of the trail the locals call The Grind.

Still I had no tears, only lightness.

When Chuck and I returned home, I placed the rock beside Dad's Navy photo, in the bookcase in our great room. Separate from the parade of heart-shaped stones lining the kitchen window, apart from the wooden bowl of heart-shaped rocks in the pantry that I use to weight vases when they are filled with tall flowers, this one was apart because I want to be able to identify this one gray rock, Dad's rock. My reminder: I am free.

For several hours I sorted through boxes of photographs, reorganizing them by time period, choosing images of Dad to scan and email to relatives. In the third hour, a small piece of white paper emerged from a disorganized stack of photos, folded in half, then in half again. Opening the unfamiliar paper, I saw my father's handwriting, the tilted scrawl with his usual misspellings and random capital letters.

Dear Elisa,

I think of the many years I spent with you.
I see what a Jewel you turned out to Be.
I can't say Enough about your work and How sweet
You realy are.

Thanks so much for all the help you did on the Lake house.

As Ever Your Loving Dad

He must have written this in the last decade, early in his Alzheimer's process, back when I worked on their lake house. Here is the validation I craved. How had I overlooked this when Dad was alive?

In Glen Ellen now, six months after the inferno, entire neighborhoods, devoid of trees, look bereft, exposed, unsheltered. Homeowners install new fences, more than there used to be, a semblance of shelter. A busy patchwork of recovery begins; foundations are staked out, concrete is poured. The landscape has changed in me too. I hope to grow into the open space created by the absence of my father. His note, written proof of his approval, provides a semblance of shelter, of acceptance, and I am grateful.

TWENTY-TWO

Rescue Me, 1972

Near the end of summer, without warning, the ashram where I lived with Jamey lost its lease. We all had a month to find a new place. Jamey and I came home one afternoon after visiting a friend for a few days to find the ashram's main house empty. Inside the office, all that remained was one lamp with no shade, an old black phone, and a list of phone numbers taped to the wall.

Wow. Now what?

Lifting the phone, I checked for a dial tone. But who to call? Not my friends at the veggie restaurant; they were all single and childless. Jamey's energy was too bright and free, not something they could appreciate on a daily basis. Anyway, I wanted to live in the country. One phone number on the list had a prefix out of the area. I didn't recognize the name beside it, but I dialed, and a man answered on the second ring.

"Hi, um, this might sound strange. You don't know me, but do you know anyone who might be looking for a roommate? We want to live in the country, and I hoped you or someone at this phone number might know of a place."

Luke was a writer. He invited me to come and look around, directing me to a lone road bisecting an ocean of rolling prairie halfway between Sacramento and Placerville. As I drove the fifteen miles, we passed a sign: Rescue, Population 68. I recalled this sign from many years ago. When we reached the turn off to Luke's place, I recognized the land. I watched for this very road whenever Dad drove the back way home from Sacramento. Magnetized by the expansive pasture and soft rolling hills, I always wondered what lay beyond. Now my old truck rambled over the crusty rutted dirt road. Jamey, three and a half, stood up on the seat and watched a cluster of oaks in the distance slowly rise higher against the horizon.

"He says the house is under the trees," I said, downshifting. We rolled on, squinting in the late afternoon sun.

The wooden farmhouse was low and small, almost a hundred years old. Luke's wiry, flyaway hair and crowded teeth went with his angsty New York voice, and we settled in the kitchen with tea to size each other up.

"I never use this bedroom off the kitchen," he said as he showed me around. The room was simple and neat, with a set of bunk beds, a double bed, and one dresser. Inside the closet hung some vintage clothes, and when I tried on a 1930s women's jacket trimmed in braid, it fit. There was nothing fizzy or edgy between Luke and me. Nothing alarming. I could tell we wouldn't have to be lovers if I decided to live here, if he let us. We went back to our tea.

A harp-like sound floated through the screen door. Out in the barn Jamey had discovered the husk of an old upright piano and was strumming the exposed strings, sending delicate notes across the rutted road, past the woodpile. The tones evaporated away and for a moment this place and all the prairie seemed empty. Devoid. Then Luke asked if I could cook. We agreed to share the house, the chores, and split the forty-dollar-a-month rent.

I was out in the yard chopping wood a few weeks later when the phone rang. Luke was calling from San Francisco. He wanted to move to the city. Would Jamey and I be all right living alone? I spun in a circle under the broad sky, opened wide my arms and bowed my thanks to God. At last I could claim my time to be a mother. No distractions. No witnesses. Time to just *be*.

We lived frugally on the monthly welfare check. Once a week, we drove into Rescue to pick up mail and shop at Howdy's Place, a small general store. One afternoon in the late fall, we removed the rubble littering the floor of the barn: muddy, torn papers and crumpled old boxes left by others long ago. Who would leave a mess like that? We put our neat cartons of books, poems, and drawings in the center so they would stay dry. One day the landlord dropped off forty shaggy red cows to graze the winter pasture. He handed a small sack of candy to Jamey out the window of his truck, and I handed him the rent. He didn't ask about Luke. We were the official hippie renters now.

My premonition of emptiness resurfaced from time to time. What were we doing here, marooned, watching winter approach? High clouds turned to dense fog; one dark afternoon our power flickered; off/on, off/on/off. Spooky. In the smelly light of the kerosene lamp, Jamey pasted strips of bright construction paper together into multicolored chains we looped all across the ceiling. A milky fog hid everything, even the low picket fence. The next day, and the next, still no power. When at last the fog lifted, I went to the utility pole and saw a clump of shaggy cow hairs on the switch box. There was no boogeyman, just an itchy cow that left us in the dark.

Like the power failure, I learned everything about the land after the fact. When the first heavy rains came, the cows disappeared. For three days we wondered where they might be until we saw some bony hips sticking out of the barn. Our boxes! Forty cows, milling in slow circles, had ground all our papers and pictures into a pile of rubble that looked very much like the trash we'd cleared three months before.

Things were not what they seemed. Perhaps we should stay through a full course of seasons before deciding what this country life meant to me, to Jamey, to us. I wrote poetry, drew pen and ink drawings, and began to sleep a lot. A musician friend asked us to keep his dog for a while, and two weeks later Fiddle surprised us with thirteen puppies. When she got a bristly sticker embedded in her chest, the vet said she could no longer nurse. Jamey and I spent mornings grinding up our stored hippie grains (millet, wheat, and rice), simmering them in goat milk, and hand-feeding the pups. I slept even more. We gave away the puppies at the annual Grange Hall pancake breakfast.

Winter brought rain, then rainstorms, and then flooding. Our road was so rutted we made a wider track in the pasture, creating alternate routes to keep from getting stuck. The cows moaned and huddled, turning their backs to the wind. I thought about fixing things like the leaky faucet dripping into the rainy weeds out back. But once I got the wood in, made our oatmeal, read to Jamey, and took a nap, it was almost time to start dinner. At night we read some more.

I decided to become more spiritual, so I studied Sufism, reading Hazrat Inayat Kahn's slim book, *The Purpose of Life*. Jamey and I threw three coins and consulted the *I Ching*—lots of times. Our favorite hexagram was Tui: the Joyous, lake. When we went on long hikes, we looked for tracks, for signs. Sometimes the sun broke through, and puddles in the red dirt road reflected a brilliant blue, dotted with white clouds. We rejoiced over the little skies floating at our feet. Windswept and soggy, we returned indoors. Winter was not even half over.

Low fog covered everything, sometimes for days. When it lifted, full color returned, and it was so psychedelic we were drunk just with seeing. One day the sun was in, then out, then in, then out. Huge dark clouds bounced around the horizon, and the songbirds were going crazy. Out beyond the barn sat a mighty chunk of rainbow, a giant square reaching clear down to the ground. Without a word we broke into a run, running for the end of that rainbow. We splashed through the puddles in our high boots, coming nearer and nearer.

Without warning it vanished.

We turned for home, happy enough to have come that close. After a bit we looked back, and there it was again! We ran straight for it, closer, closer. And once more it disappeared. Dang!

But wait—maybe we were *in* the rainbow. Damp all over from the mist, we laughed with wonder, drenched in our miracle. Maybe we were always in a rainbow and just couldn't see it.

For a lot of the time, nothing happened. I seemed sleepier, yes, poorer, for sure, but no more spiritual. By now, we wore the same clothes all week. I liked the spicy muskiness of my long velvet skirt and the vintage dresses I cut short and wore atop a leotard. I read aloud *The Yearling* and *Wind in the Willows*, *Little Bear*, and Laura Ingalls Wilder's books. When the rain finally stopped, Jamey set out on midday treks with his lunch in a sack. As long as he had on his boots and stayed in the center of the dirt road, he was safe. He said the deer came to him when he hiked out past the slow bend.

We were not really people there, alone. We were more like a piece of the place: a stone or a stick or a leaf. We were just there. As summer approached, we lived in a kind of suspended time. The days stretched long and longer still. At night, the stars were so dense they looked overdone, pretend. The prairie turned golden, and the long grass whispered in the evening wind. Daybreak was pink, and noon was white hot. We trudged through the thick red dust to the pond, tapping our sticks on the earth, watching for long compressed lines cutting across the road, snake tracks. Slipping down the mud bank, we slid quietly into the soft pond water and watched ring after golden ring open silently before us as we skimmed the surface, keeping clear of the marshy plants waving beneath. On the way home, Jamey wore only his boots, his hair shaggy-long and his skin peachy all over. My hair, a tangled bundle, dripped pond water down my back, keeping me cool. By the time we opened the gate we were both bone dry.

How could I have thought there was nothing here? The dripping faucet in the yard made a lush oasis for tree frogs. They crowded together, clinging to the cool pipe in the heat of the day. At night, the bullfrog chorus was so loud we laughed.

One morning a broad shadow fell for an instant over the kitchen window. Suddenly the yard filled with waves of bright, flittering birdsong. Our giant oak was alive with incandescent yellow birds; at the dripping faucet, they sipped, splashed, and sang. The yard and the sky were filled with intense, insistent yellow. Hundreds of tiny migrating birds had found our lone leaky faucet in the middle of nowhere. An hour later, they were gone.

As summer wound down, I began to dread the isolation of winter. Was this my life, watching time slip by? Instead of taking naps, I raged around cleaning things, sorting through the rubble in the barn. I put fresh paint on the front half of the house, swept the path, and raked the yard. I soaked our white clothes in bleach and brushed and brushed my bundle of tangled hair until it was smooth again and long.

The winds gusted; the days grew short; the sun weakened.

I had pushed and pulled and clipped and snipped and swept everything within reach. On Halloween night, with Jamey asleep in his bed, the woodstove warmed the room with an even heat. Wind-whipped branches danced against the roof, and the eerie, uneven swishing made me jumpy, wild.

I leapt up, grabbed a sweater and strode into the night toward the horizon, the one place with a view toward Sacramento. Pale grasses reflected the light of a huge moon. Everything seemed to glow. Through the pasture, past sleepy cows, I made my way up to the crest of the hill to find the lights of the city below me.

I flung wide my arms and bellowed, "Okay. I am *done* with this! If I'm so spiritual, why am I hiding here?"

Wind whipped my hair and skirt. I stood tall and let it blow straight through me.

"Okay, God. I'll go to the city. I will work hard and support my son. I will *make* my life, but I need something from you. I need a place to live that feels safe—and real. Not an apartment and not with my mother. Just give me that by Christmas, and I will do the rest."

I stomped away, down the long hill, past the cows to the kitchen door, and stood in the yellow circle of light in the familiar wooden room. Faded paper chains, dusty with cobwebs, cluttered half the ceiling. Taking a clean sheet of paper, I wrote out my deal with God. I was no longer angry.

The very next day, we started planning for our move. We had plenty of paper and fabric and a sewing machine. It would cost almost nothing to create inventory for a holiday craft fair near downtown Sacramento. When our friend returned to retrieve his dog, he put together a booth that I painted to look like an old cabin. In early December, Jamey and I spent our days selling my hand-lettered, illustrated children's story, *Little Wave*, and kid-sized corduroy craft aprons, tied with velvet ribbon, with pockets holding six fat crayons. The craft fair lasted two weeks. We sold everything.

One day a man stopped by our booth. He said he'd heard he should meet me because I was so creative. I only half listened. He was just a guy. He wanted to show me his restoration project, a vintage house next to a park in Sacramento. Would we come over?

We went. David's half-remodeled, old two-story house was in an Italian neighborhood in the heart of Sacramento. In the back, across a deep lawn, was a small cottage. When we were touring the yard with David, the current renter stood on the threshold of the little wooden place, arms crossed, proprietary. I didn't mention wanting to live there, but it was perfect.

In the early afternoon the day before Christmas, a mutual friend drove up to our gate. Curious, Jamey and I came out and stood beside the low picket fence.

"Hey Elisa, David just called. He said to tell you the cottage in the back is available. Do you and Jamey want to move in tomorrow?" We took him up on this offer.

Our time in Rescue changed me. There, Jamey and I discovered the scent of grass when the dew burned off, the high afternoon hum of summer grasshoppers, and the mighty roar of bullfrogs. We danced in a rainbow and watched a thousand finches singing, then walked under a million stars. We were golden. We were known. I was not alone.

It's haunting, my memory of those plain, uninterrupted days. I'd return there for another course of seasons if I could. Today our prairie is covered in houses; all thousand acres are paved. The rutted red dirt road with the slow bend, where the deer came to Jamey, remains only a mark on this page. Our time alone together in Rescue saved me. At last I found kinship, a human I could trust—my son.

TWENTY-THREE

Sacramento,
the 1970s

When Jamey and I left Rescue for Sacramento, reentering civilization was not difficult. At the end of our street, a grassy park included one giant, shaggy cedar tree with branches evenly spaced, almost like a ladder. From our lookout near the top, Jamey and I could see everything, even the Mormon church and basketball courts that bordered the far side. We had our cozy cottage. My deal with God was working out. We were safe.

Jamey and I were busier than we had been for a year. I got a job as a baker in a nearby restaurant, where I met Monica, a thin young woman in her early twenties. Within days, I was mortified to find myself deep in my one and only girl crush. Tracking her whereabouts in the restaurant kitchen, I made up reasons to be near her. I wanted to be as close as possible to her fine, pale skin. At night, I pictured the delicate blue veins near her collarbone. Monica, the actual whole person, was incidental and didn't figure in my fantasy. It was just her skin . . . I was relieved when, within two weeks, my obsession subsided. It seemed a good time to end my experiment with celibacy.

I went to Planned Parenthood; preventing pregnancy was key. Birth control pills made me emotional and puffy, which seemed like a bad tradeoff. The doctor attempted to insert an IUD but gave up after twenty minutes. I was not a good candidate. When he brought in a box full of large surgical rubber discs for a diaphragm fitting, I sat up, took my feet out of the stirrups, and prepared to leave. "There is no way I want to smell like surgical rubber, and those are *all* too big. A diaphragm is *out*."

I decided to have a tubal ligation. Because I was only twenty-two, it took two months to convince the doctor of my certainty.

The night before the surgery, David came to visit me, along with Eddie, his partner in the house restoration project. They asked if I would someday regret "shutting the door," but neither had raised a child. Eddie, a lanky, open, funny guy in his mid-twenties, suggested we "talk this out," which did not surprise me since he had a degree in psychology. But I knew every two years, like clockwork, an intense desire to have another baby permeated everything I did, despite the fact that I had zero desire to raise more children. This "baby fever" seemed hormonal, somehow instinctual, and not in any way practical. Ironclad prevention was the wisest course. I went ahead with the procedure, though many times after that I felt varying degrees of regret.

Remodeling was new to all of us, and the process was more or less democratic. As work progressed on the main house, I helped hang wallpaper and did most of the prep and painting. I chose paint and tile colors and helped refinish floors. I liked working with paint; they liked working with lumber and any task that made lots of noise. I cooked at the restaurant until two each day while Eddie and David did loud and dusty construction. Then I would sand or paint. Almost every evening Jamey and I went to the park to swing on the swings or climb the broad cedar tree.

On the first day of kindergarten, he marched up the sidewalk and into the classroom, curious and willing. He was ready.

Soon after Jamey started school, Eddie and I discussed becoming more than friends. We were attracted to each other but didn't want to mess up our working relationship. Also, Eddie was, as he put it, "not ready to step in as someone's father." I would never welcome anyone stepping in, or on, my parenting role. We reached an agreement, a rendition of "friends with benefits." But once we began having sex, I loved the closeness, the connection. I wanted it to last.

In the '70s, feminism, equality, and "woman power" resonated with me. After all, I always believed I was a person first. Of course a woman can do anything a man can do. But why then did I feel diminished when a man chose *not* to marry me? Just as my mother, who now had her master's degree in psychology, had warned, my self-esteem seemed tied to the approval of men. I managed to identify this weakness, but awareness is just the first step in making a change. Instead of broadening the ways I could affirm myself, I punted. I refrained from pressing for marriage.

David and Eddie's remodeling project sold right away for full price. Eddie and I became partners on a second house a few blocks from Jamey's school. Power struggles emerged over two things—parenting Jamey and design aesthetics. We successfully hammered and plastered our way through twelve houses in five short years and learned to work around our continuing differences. My mother did not approve of my casual hippie lifestyle. In her view, finishing college was the path to success. My independent work life—with no benefits, no insurance, and self-styled goals—made her uneasy.

"If you got a job at the post office, you would have benefits and security," she suggested. I dismissed her conventional ideas, but I did appreciate her companionship with my son.

Mom and Jamey loved going to Lawrence Livermore National Laboratory and the Exploratorium in San Francisco. Mom's husband, Jack, took Jamey flying in his small plane and to an outdoor shooting range. They gave me the money to buy a used upright piano, and Jamey started piano lessons and swimming lessons. Though our home life in a remodeling project was chaotic, Jamey lilted along.

Eddie seemed to resent my son's freewheeling childhood and attempted to impose rules that neither Jamey nor I appreciated. Some of the rules we adopted, like the paper route, and some I vetoed. If Eddie's design idea or new childrearing rule met with resistance, he sulked. Power struggles were inevitable, and each of the three of us found ways to disengage, to reassert our individuality.

I was surprised when Jamey found a church near every place we lived. He tried Catholic mass with Eddie's parents when he was six and at seven attended a Baptist church every summer Sunday with a family across the street. When he turned eight, we moved to a beautiful vintage brick house a couple of doors away from a Quaker meeting house. One day as we were sitting outside in the sun, I asked Jamey which church he liked the best. I was curious why he was drawn to religious services. Was it structure he was looking for? More belonging?

"Well, the Mormon church has basketball, and they have a big choir. Brother Andy at the Baptist church did a lot of yelling, but the singing was really good. At the Catholic church, everyone has to kneel and stand, only one guy does all the talking, and there's no singing. But at the Quaker church, they call you friend, and anyone can say anything they want. Plus, they sent me a thank you card in the mail, even though we live across the street. So the Quaker church is my favorite." Perhaps my son longed for both structure and belonging.

Through the first three years with Eddie, my unwavering desire for marriage simmered on the back burner. Finally Eddie capitulated. Dad and his new wife, Marsha, hosted a traditional wedding and reception at their country club. Jamey, at six and a half, walked me down the aisle.

Soon after the honeymoon, Eddie began sitting alone on the front porch most evenings, strumming melancholy guitar chords. Before long, he booked carpentry and design jobs on his own, away from me. He was not settling into marriage. When I planted a garden, put up veggies, and baked bread, he grumbled that I was "too wife-y."

To ease my worries and gain perspective, I took up running, a new fad in 1976. My long trail runs along the river outside Sacramento buoyed my sense of self but increased the distance between us. I arranged some publicity for our historic restoration company, an idea I got from Grandma Bishop. Almost every week, when I was little, a few lines were printed in the small local paper about my grandmother—her charity work or some trip she had taken. "They don't know what to print if you don't tell them," she claimed. When Eddie and I were featured on the front page of the Home section of the Sacramento newspaper, Eddie accused me of flaunting my star quality. The article focused on a woman in a man's world rather than us as partners. I had no intention of stealing his limelight; the reporter just took that angle. Women in construction were rare in the 1970s.

"You know what they say—the cream rises to the top, right?" he said in a derisive tone as he refolded the paper with a crisp crack and set it down.

Somehow everything became a contest. We worked full time on restoration, doing two houses at a time now, doubling our investment almost like clockwork. Jamey worked with us after school, on weekends, summers; by the time he was seven, he was removing and replacing hardware, sanding, and sweeping. He watched me hang wallpaper, choose colors, and grout tile.

While Eddie and I learned the ins and outs of construction and real estate, we also started using the 1970s drug of choice: cocaine. A friend returned from Peru with two pounds of pure cocaine in his backpack, hidden inside a sack of dog food—his ploy to get through customs. He brought his entire backpack, minus the kibble, to our half-finished project. Eddie was all for trying it. I watched him snort a line and then shake his head, eyes wide.

"Wow, that burns. Whoa. My brain just cranked up four notches."

Curious, I tried a couple of lines. Within minutes we were striding around, captivated by the rapid-fire surge of ideas the cocaine unleashed. Our emotional differences were masked by the drug. Soon we bought a small amount of cocaine every week or two because we wanted to party, or because we were tired, or just because we were bored. Why worry? We tried mushrooms and peyote, but we preferred cocaine. Besides, it was hip. Sophisticated. Everyone was doing it. Right?

We bought a dump truck. Eddie took up flying. We bought a small plane. We traveled with Jamey to New York City and Disneyland. Through all this, Eddie remained conflicted about marriage.

"I do eventually want to have a child," he said when pressed about our future. "And I don't want to adopt."

"Well, geez, Eddie, what's the basis for staying married if deep down you want something you know full well I can never give you?"

We separated and regrouped a number of times. We liked the stimulation, intensity, and success of our work and our sexual connection. Deeper intimacy eluded us, though what I shared with Eddie was richer than any previous relationship.

We tried couples counseling. When asked to list what we each wanted from an ideal relationship, I showed up toting four pages of yellow legal paper listing mental, emotional, physical, and spiritual qualities. Eddie dug a scrap of paper out of his pocket, and read one sentence,

"Locks doors and opens cereal boxes correctly."

Really.

Eddie and I stopped seeing each other and prepared to divorce. The morning I told Jamey we would be living alone again, he asked, "Mom, can we have a meeting? I mean, even sit down?"

This was a big deal. Most of the time we were in motion— off to swimming lessons, painting a room, or running with the dog down by the river. Across the side driveway next to our brick house, the neighbor practiced classical piano, and on this day Baroque chords drifted across the alley into our dining room, mixing with the patterned wallpaper and period style furniture. The notes floated around us, a Bartok soundtrack.

"We keep changing our name, you know?" Jamey said. "We've had a lot of last names."

Sitting up straight at the polished mahogany table, pants belted, polo shirt tucked in tight, Jamey no doubt craved something consistent, buttoned down, neat, and straight. Did I mention he was only eight?

"Well, yeah, we have had a lot of names."

"What if we picked one and just used that from now on, you know, no matter what?" he asked.

The earnest little guy was growing so fast there was a faint metallic smell to him, like he was being manufactured right there in front of me. He watched me, his shoulders a little high.

"Okay, let's look at our last names," I suggested. We counted them off, my maiden name, his father's last name, Eddie's last name . . . "Which one do you like best?" I asked.

"I like your original name," he said plainly.

We agreed to stick with Stancil—no matter what.

"We will be our own family, Jamey. Small but mighty," I reassured him.

TWENTY-FOUR

Pollyanna,
1977

When Eddie moved out, we divided our business holdings. I kept the renovated vintage brick house, a small truck, and the painting equipment. Eddie took the rest. I was twenty-seven. I decreased cocaine and increased distance running. Skimming along the narrow trail beside the American River, I could run three, seven, even eleven miles, feeling strong and free. The trail meandered along the outskirts of Sacramento, and Jamey and our big German shepherd, Pappy, came along sometimes.

One Saturday in April 1977, Jamey and I decided to celebrate a landmark event. For the first time, I was filing taxes as a single, successful business woman. After swinging by the post office, we visited an older woman Jamey met when we lived near the Mormon church. He liked to play piano for her sometimes. Then we went to the river with Pappy. After a short run, we planned to have dinner at our favorite pizza place.

At the river, there were just a few cars parked near the path to the beach. The afternoon sun was bright, but it was early spring. Sunset would be early. Jamey decided to stay on the sandy shore and skip rocks with Pappy while I ran a twenty-minute victory lap just a mile downriver.

About a half mile into the run, I heard the sound of a motorbike. This was odd because motorbikes were not allowed on the trails. I spotted the guy a few hundred yards away, up on the levee. He began to ride parallel to me along the levee. At about a mile, I stopped, took off my long-sleeved top and tied it around my waist. As I turned to run back, I heard the trail bike cutting across a sandy hill, heading for the lower trail. My trail.

There was a steep cliff on my left, and to my right a hedge of dense bramble branches grew along the sandbank. I picked up my pace. The motorbike came closer, louder. I stopped. If this guy was weird I planned to confront him, not be run over from behind.

"Um, no motorbikes are allowed on this trail. You might not realize that," I said as the stocky rider pulled to a stop beside me. His helmet's full-face shield reflected the late sun, but I could see the kid was about fifteen. He wore a heavy ski jacket and gloves, though it was warm out.

In a thick voice he asked, "Uhhh . . . can you tell me where *pear-dice* beach is at?" Paradise Beach was just below where I parked my car. Paradise Beach was where Jamey was playing with our dog.

"Sure," I said in a bright voice. "You need to go back up to the levee road where you were. Up ahead you just turn left and follow the levee; you will come to the parking lot. There are people there, lots of cars." I marked the directions with big arm movements, hoping to be understood. I could tell from just one glance that he was mentally slow.

"Bye," I said, then continued running up the trail toward Jamey with an even, speedy pace. I heard the motorbike behind me. I crossed the side path that led to the levee. He did not take that path.

He was closing in.

The cliff bordering the river to my left was high and steep. The thick brush on my right gave me only one choice: run faster. Determined to make it back to Jamey, I ran faster and faster, but the motorbike was on me, too close, too fast.

A vapor of pure fear rose up, stealing my breath, and like Peter Rabbit, I dived sideways into the brambles, screaming as loudly as I could as I tumbled into the brush. The guy dumped his motorcycle and leapt onto me, dropping me downhill through the branches into a low swale of sand. In an instant, both of his elbows pinned me, cutting into my biceps; his heavy trunk lay across my hips; his hands encircled my neck. My nails broke as I clawed at his thick nylon jacket. I released a strangled scream.

"Shut *up*," he said. "*Shut up shut up* or I'll kill you," he grunted, spitting out the words. I couldn't breathe; more screaming was impossible. I began to black out. As my vision darkened, I glanced up at the rim of the sand bank where a solitary blade of oat grass wavered in the breeze, scribbling in the wind against the evening sky.

Then a large tennis shoe, a man's tennis shoe, appeared on the bank.

"Hey, what are you doing?"

Oh no. Was this his friend?

"Get off her right *now*," Tennis Shoe Guy said. When the attacker leaned back, up and off of me, I drew a deep breath and crab scrambled sideways and away.

"Get him! He is trying—I think he's trying to kill me!" I yelled as I stood.

Just then a fisherman appeared, pole in hand, clambering up the steep cliff from the river below. As I ran off, I heard him tell the boy very slowly and clearly, "You are in a lot of trouble now. Get your motorbike. You have to come with us."

Alarm rang through me as I wobbled down the trail, tears streaming. Where was my mighty power? Where was my son? How could I have left him alone?

I tore across the beach calling for Jamey, my voice ragged and hoarse, unable to meter my terror. Together we ran to the nearest house and banged on the door, Pappy on our heels. I felt stripped bare, raw. An older couple hovered near the door. I asked them to call the police. Jamey and I waited in the car, and Pappy's dog breath steamed the windows as waves of shock spread over me. Jamey stayed quiet, petting the dog. The police soon arrived and within minutes the Fisherman, Tennis Shoe Guy, and at last the attacker, methodically pushing his trail bike, came into view. Off to one side, the police took Polaroid photos of my red and abraded neck and the scrapes and bruises on my arms and legs. I could not look at that boy. I was shaking and weak. Jamey stood with his hands clenched, staring him down.

We went straight home. No pizza. No celebration for being a successful single business woman. Instead I paced across the antique Chinese, hand-hooked rug in our apricot living room, feeling exposed and afraid. I wanted only to huddle down and hide.

I had bruises and a broken voice for two weeks. When I testified in court a few months later, the young deputy district attorney was so nervous he sweated and trembled visibly as he questioned me on the stand, attempting to set the scene. He repeatedly asked me how high the grass was and what I was wearing. Frustrated, I finally said, "Look, I was attacked, and I screamed. If you want me to demonstrate my scream I am happy to do so right now."

The judge cautioned me, saying, "Ms. Stancil, you are not to speak freely."

The boy sat in court with his mother, a squat woman with

a faint mustache. The two lived across the river in a poor part of town where he had previously been arrested for receiving stolen property. His defense? My loud screams scared him; he was trying to get me to stop. I never checked back to find out the sentence he received. His future was bleak no matter the trial outcome.

Of course, everyone knows a woman running alone is vulnerable. I had a plan, just outrun anyone who tried to harm me. But in real life, real harm overpowered me, and the only thing that saved me was my scream. What other clever plans of mine, crafted to guarantee safety and freedom, might be just as flimsy, nothing more than Pollyanna schemes?

For the next few years I joined the merry-go-round of runners circling the eight-block park nearest our house. For years running alone was not comfortable. To protect myself now I stay vigilant, I carry a phone, I share my route, and manage to feel the bliss of running free about half the time.

TWENTY-FIVE

Fragile Interconnections, 1978

I n 1978 I took classes in creative writing and communication at University of California, Davis. Before long I called *Sacramento Magazine*, citing my remodeling work and claiming I had done "some writing." I got a call back from the editor.

"Come in this afternoon with some examples of your work, and we can talk."

I was terrified. My work had been published, but only in the six-page literary magazine I had started at community college. Quickly rolling fresh paper into my black Olivetti, I typed one pithy and ironic paragraph about Sacramento's reputation as a cow town. And on a second page, two paragraphs in a straight journalistic style about home restoration. Searching my wardrobe for something writer-ish, I settled for jeans, a button-down shirt and a brown linen jacket. When I met the editor, he had on jeans, a blue shirt, and a brown linen sports coat. So far, so good. He scanned my two offerings. Looking up without saying anything about the writing, he said, "We need a home and garden editor for a piece on homes of ten movers and shakers in Sacramento, with interviews, featuring the architecture as well. Would you like to do it?"

This assignment was a ten-page feature article, the cover story. After the brief thrill of seeing my byline in print, I realized journalism was not a gold mine. During the next year and a half I wrote about medicine, creative financing, public education, and home decor: basically, whatever they wanted or I was interested in. I wrote for various publications for two years, but real money was easier to make in home remodeling.

I sold the vintage brick house and bought a contemporary four-bedroom ranch-style house I could update on my own with paint and wallpaper. Jamey helped me tear out hideous orange shag carpeting and cheap sheets of dark walnut paneling. I patched and painted and shifted the energy of the house, inside and out. I also partnered on a big Italianate estate with Bill, a young real estate mogul I interviewed for my first feature article on "movers and shakers."

Busy with writing, running and remodeling, I dated, but no one special. Jamey started at Country Day, a private school, and decided to change his first name to James. *The Bionic Woman* was a new show, and the main character was a young woman named Jamie. My son did not want a girl's name.

Concerns about status surfaced at Country Day, affecting James's sense of self. His new friends had swimming pools, televisions mounted on their bedroom walls, and extra houses in Tahoe and Hawaii. "Look, James," I reassured him, "your friends have parents twenty years older than me. Most of them are almost fifty. They have had more time to build wealth. We can catch up, but it will take some time."

My partner Bill introduced me to his loan officer at a local savings and loan. I leveraged two properties with short-term, interest-only loans. Balloon payments would come due within two years, but that was no big deal. Why worry? I was smart, I was skilled, and I was lucky. Every project sold within the first week on the market, for the full asking price, without a real estate agent. I had a system.

At twenty-eight, I was fit, happy, more or less solvent, and lonely. In the early spring, Bill introduced me to Harry, a good friend from Oakland. Harry worked in remodeling and design and joined the team on the big house. He was creative, warm, and brilliant. He knew who he was and what he wanted. Harry was the first grown up man I dated. I fell hard.

We went to romantic dinners and took short weekend trips to the wine country. About once a week James, Harry, and I went to Bill's impressive house on a tree-lined street two blocks from our work site. We were welcome anytime to swim and barbeque. Near Bill's front door, a dense row of leafy rose bushes created a tall hedge. Harry would cut one buttery yellow rose, remove the thorns, and give it to me on our way in. One day, handing me a rose, he said, "See? I am taming you, like in *The Little Prince*. One rose at a time."

By early summer we were living together and planned to buy a project to remodel together. Work was continuing apace, and, despite nearing loan deadlines, everything was lining up. We now spent every day and night together. Harry was the youngest of five brothers, raised by a single mother, so he knew how to treat an eleven-year-old part boy/part young man like James. They roughhoused in the pool and talked about surfing and bikes. When Harry was around, James felt free to play intense stride and blues piano riffs as loud as he did when he was alone.

Harry was set to crew on a sailboat to Hawaii, a plan he'd had for a year. He would be gone for weeks. A few days before he was to sail, he had some business in the Bay Area and planned to stay the night with friends. This was the first night in a long time we would be apart. We spent the morning grouting Italian tile at the big project, laughing and goofing around.

"You know, last night was the *first* time you turned to me in your sleep and held me close," he said, touching my cheek, leaving a little grout print. "I think you are finally beginning to trust me."

Washing up, he checked his watch then said, "I have to hurry to beat the traffic." A quick kiss goodbye and down the stairs he raced.

Leaning out the upstairs window, I called down, "Harry, you told me to remind you of something, but I don't remember what it is."

"Don't worry, I don't remember either. I'll see you tomorrow. We have to sign the papers on the new house at Bill's first thing in the morning." And with that he drove away.

After dinner that night, James and I worked in the yard. Soon this house would be on the market. I thought of calling Harry to say goodnight, but intruding on his free night seemed needy. If he wanted to call, he would call. The phone remained silent.

At five thirty in the morning I awakened in a panic. Something was wrong. Harry!

Just then the phone began to ring, and I grabbed it, expecting to hear his voice.

"Elisa . . ." It was Bill, calling so early.

"Bill, is Harry already there?"

"Yes, um, come on over. I'm making coffee," he said, and hung up.

I didn't take the time to leave a note; I rushed out without waking my son. As I drove the mile and a half in the early morning air, I applied a little blush, a little lipstick. I remember thinking I might have to go to the hospital. Hoping I would be that lucky.

At Bill's, I parked and ran straight across the deep front lawn, through the tall hedge of roses. One of the blooming yellow roses caught on my blouse, a large thorn momentarily holding me there. With care, I gently released it. Filled with woe I stepped into the formal front hall. There stood only Bill. No Harry.

"Elisa . . . I . . . Look, Elisa, Harry is dead. He died in a car accident an hour ago."

We don't fully grasp the fragile crystalline framework we have built, the transparent interconnections between what is *now* and what we assume will follow. The breathtaking scale of our expectation is most evident when everything disintegrates, in a heartbeat, after hearing just one word.

Death? I thought I knew what to do. When the baby died, I promised next time I faced this kind of loss I would *not* hold on, instead just scream out the pain right away, just scream it all out. The fact that someone lived is so much more important than the fact that they died. I would honor life, not mourn death. This was my plan.

I ran past Bill to the powder room and closed the door. As I leaned into the doorjamb, I gathered up a guest towel to muffle my scream, but no sound would come. Inside was only emptiness. In the face of this terrible news, a high hiss of near silence sounded the alarm. I had no special powers, no insights, no solutions. I sank deep into uncharted waters.

When Harry left the morning before, I was supposed to remind him to get gas. There was a gas shortage, and we knew there would be long lines; most gas stations would be closed at night. But I forgot.

Harry's friends said that night he laughed and asked, "What am I doing here with you guys when I could be with her?" Instead of staying the night, he headed back. About thirty minutes from my house, he took a side road, probably searching for a gas station. When his car stalled, out of gas, he pulled over and put on flashers. The highway patrol said the drunk driver plowed into Harry's car, then into Harry, hitting with such force he was thrown fifty feet. He died on the way to the hospital.

The teenaged driver was arrested for drunk driving, driving a stolen truck, and driving with a suspended license (for two previous drunk driving violations).

The sun was up at Bill's house, lighting the lemon trees, the roses, and jasmine. Workers would soon arrive at my job site. Too confounded to drive, I walked the few blocks to meet the subcontractors to tell them what happened. The main painter offered to take care of things for the next two weeks. I called James and asked him to ride his bike over. Asking him to travel to bad news seemed unfair, but then everything seemed unfair. When he arrived, I told him with gentle words, one hand on his shoulder, one on the center of his back. I held on.

This loss was my son's first experience with death. In a combined state of wonder and despair, James was quiet as he stood by me throughout that day. He was beside me when I called the morgue and asked to speak to "someone, hopefully a woman, who handles the bodies."

"Hello. My fiancé is there with you. His name is Harry Blackwell. Um, have you seen him? And if you have, could you tell me, as a woman . . . do you think I should come down there?" I knew I would regret it if I didn't at least try to be with him one last time.

There was a long pause on the line.

"I understand you want to say goodbye, but no . . . no, I would not come down," she said with a gentle voice.

"He was a beautiful man, wasn't he?" I asked.

"Yes, yes, he was," she agreed.

Back at the house, I opened the refrigerator to make lunch for James and there, wrapped in plastic, was the vibrant spinach I bought yesterday for tonight's dinner. Spinach, so *alive*. I closed the door and leaned against it. When James saw me falter, he asked, "What should we do now, Mom?"

"Now we have to keep moving, James. Just keep moving. Let's get the push mower and mow and mow the lawn in front and the lawn in back, then rake and rake. We will keep moving until I can stand to stay still."

TWENTY-SIX

Losing,
1979–1984

There is no insurance against emotional pain. Despite whatever pain we have already survived, loss carves out a new emptiness each time. After the funeral, James stayed with a friend for four days. I bought some cocaine, determined to focus, to write out everything I remembered about Harry. Typing on onionskin with my new IBM Selectric, my fingers shook as I used more and more cocaine, staying up, typing through the night into dawn. I still have these fifty sheets of semi-transparent paper, stored away, with a photo of Harry taken while he was sailing off the coast of Brazil.

Before we met I bought some thick, soft gray towels, thinking one day I would wrap these around my new man—a new man who would treasure me, maybe even buy me perfume. When Harry first took a shower at my house, he emerged from the bath with one of my gray towels as big as an elephant ear draped around his shoulders. "Hey, I was at Macy's and saw these same towels in emerald green. I was thinking of buying them, but not for me. I must have been channeling you before we even met." One day he surprised me with a bottle of *Bal a Versailles* perfume. "I like it because it's strong and exotic, like you," he said. Me? Exotic?

Now I wrapped myself in the towels. I doused myself with the perfume. But he was gone.

On the fourth day, I put the writing away. I went back to running. I went back to work. The loss of Harry tested all my theories. I reminded myself it was more important to have been loved than to have lost the love, more important that someone had lived than that they had died. But this did little to counterbalance grief.

All was flatness now. Almost every day I used cocaine. The intensity of the drug helped me focus on tasks I had no heart to face. I sensed I was sinking into a dangerous pattern but each week I purchased a new supply. My four-bedroom house sold right away, and it appeared I would be able to make my way financially. When running at the park in the months that followed, I would ponder how fragile one's hold on life can be. Sun, then shade. Warm and cool. Harry here, now gone.

A few months later my younger brother Ed introduced me to Dean, an artist in Sonoma. We shared a strong interest in historical buildings and decided to partner on a remodeling project in Sacramento. Dean was living in the shadow of grief, dealing with his wife's terminal illness. Perhaps this new project would be an escape for both of us. He offered to invest $20,000, so I signed papers on one more house to remodel with him. But when the savings and loan crisis occurred, interest rates on mortgages shot up to 18 percent. All mortgages in my name were short term and tied to the prevailing interest rate. Real estate sales plummeted nationwide.

I was in deep financial trouble. James and I moved to the smallest house, one that would take the fewest resources to prepare for sale. Dean never came through with his share of the money, so that house sat nearly finished and empty. And the big Italianate project with Bill was finished but garnered not a single offer.

Over the next few months, multiple house payments, tuition at Country Day, and my continued cocaine use depleted my savings. I saw no way out. Writing an article for a few hundred dollars or painting a few rooms for cash would not cut it. I owed big. Hounded by collection agents, I turned to a consumer credit counselor. All my credit cards were destroyed, and once a week I was required to deliver cash in person, money that was then distributed to my creditors. To file bankruptcy cost five hundred dollars back then, which seemed a cruel irony since I did not have five hundred dollars to spare. Desperate to raise cash, hoping at least one house would sell, I began selling my jewelry, stereo, desk, typewriter, washer, dryer, refrigerator, and at the very end, even James's much loved piano. What would Harry think of me, now?

I relinquished the unfinished house to the bank. It was improved significantly, so there was no foreclosure. I bowed out of the big project with Bill, foregoing any share of eventual profit because I couldn't help with carrying costs. The house James and I lived in would be foreclosed.

Though others were caught in the savings and loan debacle, I felt wholly responsible for my business failure. All those years working in real estate never felt speculative. You buy a place, you improve it, and you sell it. Now, penniless and facing foreclosure, in full view of my twelve-year-old son, my shame was palpable.

Although Dean hadn't come up with $20,000 as promised, he agreed we could move into his big house in Sonoma. Sonoma seemed like the perfect place to hide.

James was disconsolate. He had full awareness of our sudden poverty. Financial loss stripped away his school, his friends, and especially his piano, all losses beyond his power to fix. Before our impending move, we went to Sonoma to check out the town. As we walked through the grass in the quaint town square, James stayed silent, his jaw set tight. He had already asked four times if there could be another choice for us.

"Why do we have to come here? We don't know anybody here."

"I am so sorry, James. This is going to be for the best even though we can't see it right now. After Harry died, I made bad decisions, and I'm really sorry. I hope you can find some good friends and be happy in your new school."

He quickly looked away to hide his welling tears. We trudged together through the rose garden, past the duck pond, in the soft shade of mature trees and palms. Just then a big bird poop fell out of the sky and plopped onto the center of James's forehead. He looked startled and deeply offended. Then he burst out laughing.

"Welcome to Sonoma, right?" he said.

"Yeah, looks like you got the official town greeting," I replied as I gently wiped away the poop. My son's ability to find humor in the midst of all this loss was impressive. Maybe we could make our way here, after all.

Dean's house was a rambling historic home with an acre of lawn, a large pool, redwoods, and in the front yard a giant palm tree. James had a room and bathroom downstairs, and there was a piano in the parlor. Not *his* piano, but at least a piano.

In Sonoma, I took any painting work I could find, even painting the exterior of a ten-unit, two-story condominium by myself, with just a ladder, a roller, and a brush. I slowly built a minor painting business and got credit at a tiny paint store on the outskirts of town. James, now in seventh grade, made a good friend whose mother worked at the local bank. She helped me get a credit card by impounding $500 and issuing a card with a $500 credit limit. It took years to regain good credit.

I painted the exterior and most of the rooms of Dean's house, and we maintained a distant, vague connection. Dean was extremely depressed after his wife died and seemed likely to stay that way. He was a gifted artist, but stalled by misery. There was not much intersection between us aside from grief. We were each immersed in making it through the day, the week, the month. Covertly, I made a monthly delivery of a large quantity of cocaine to a dealer a mile and a half away. In trade, I received a small amount of drugs.

When I saw my father and his wife, Marsha, later that year, they were concerned by my thin frame. My drug habit was starting to show. I made a pact with myself. If anyone asked if I was using drugs, I had to tell them the truth—and then quit. Right then. But I rarely stood still long enough for anyone to ask me anything.

At a restaurant in Sonoma, Dad asked if I was okay. I barked at him, "I'm fine, I'm working hard, and running a lot, that's all."

"Well, daughter, you look like something's wrong with you. You sure you are all right?"

"I'm sure," I said, leaping up to pay the bill. I would do anything to escape confrontation.

Mom was finishing her PhD and she and Jack didn't visit often, but when they did, she stayed out of my line of fire. I had become short-tempered and judgmental, and my anger made her uncomfortable. Her discomfort made me even angrier. She focused on James, and every few weeks he would go to her house with one of his friends to swim, hang out at the mall, and go to the movies.

When James was fifteen, he got a job at the local grocery store. His schoolwork seemed to be going fine. He said he was studying, and I took his word for it. One evening near the end of his sophomore year in high school, I heard a strange sound out in the backyard. Looking out the kitchen window across the deep lawn, I saw James sitting on a stone bench at the border of the property and realized the odd sound was my son—he was crying. I went out there. He held up his report card, and I saw an F and two D's.

"I was thinking of running away, but only got as far as Little Switzerland," he said. Little Switzerland was Geezerville, a rundown dinner and polka joint alongside the creek about half a mile away. James managed a sad smile. Clearly, he had no plan and needed help. We began working with Valerie, an educational counselor. She pointed out the need for structured study time, real review of homework, and more involvement from me. We used her techniques, but structure was more difficult for me to adhere to than it was for James.

Let's be clear: when meeting with Valerie I was intent on hiding my own drug use. So, we all had secrets. James was not studying, I was using drugs, and Dean was mired in depression.

Late one afternoon that spring while I was wearily shopping for some soothing body lotion at a store called Body and Soul, a woman acquaintance ambled over and struck up a conversation. After a brief visit, she suggested I read a book that had helped her: *You Can Heal Your Life*, by Louise Hay.

"What! You think my whole life is *sick*? Thanks a lot." I stomped out of the store to avoid hearing that dreaded question, "Are you using drugs?" But a week later I bought a copy of the book. At the same store, I bought *Creative Visualization* by Shakti Gawain. These books sat unopened on my nightstand while I continued using drugs. Drugs were my shield, but by now I was unclear what I was protecting myself from.

James came into the kitchen late one night and saw me pretending to read the classified ads in our small-town paper. I sat up straight and warily looked his way. He walked over and lifted the edge of the newspaper, exposing a bindle of folded paper with white powder in it.

"What's that?" he asked in an even tone.

"I . . . uh, that's coke. I've been using drugs pretty much since Harry died. Look, James . . ."

He turned away, totally disgusted, and started to leave the room, then turned back. "What are you going to do now?" he said.

"I am going to quit. Honest. In three days. I have some things to set up first. I'll probably need to rest for at least two weeks. Plus, to be totally honest, I don't want to throw this out."

"Yeah, right," he said as he walked out of the room.

"I really am going to quit. You'll see. Trust me," I said to the empty doorway.

As I pondered the best approach, it became clear the little bindle I was hoarding had to go. O-U-T. Down the toilet it went. I breathed and felt relieved. Scared. Exposed. At daybreak I made a run to the grocery store and cleared my schedule for the coming three weeks.

Upstairs in the vintage bathroom, I began filling the long, old-fashioned, claw-foot tub. After undressing, I turned off the water, tested the temperature, then stood in the center of the room. Imagining those years of drug behavior as a kind of cloak, I searched for a way to remove it, to let it go. I had forgotten how to just be me. Reaching to my neck, I untied an invisible ribbon and imagined the heavy cloak of shame dropping to the floor. I stepped into the deep tub. The water warmed me as I began to cry, sinking deep underwater so no one would hear me wail. Later in my bed, every movement triggered slivers of ice. Glacial chills of frosty despair registered in every muscle and every vein. This was a different kind of wail, a primordial echo of the physical and psychic cellular debt my drug use had created. Days and nights passed without much measurable improvement.

James was suspicious, guarded, and peeved. He was entitled to all that. In the weeks that followed, I began to reassemble myself, but he remained distant. In the garden one morning, I saw a rose. I mean *really* saw that there was a rose there, nodding in my direction. Cradling the crimson bloom, breathing in the scent, I realized in that instant that shielding myself from pain and shame, from the loss of Harry and the failure of my business, had blocked my pathway to joy. Living a lie would never heal me.

The third week, I took up the *Heal Your Life* and *Visualization* books, reading a page here or there. I slept more than twelve hours a day and only did household chores as needed. I stayed as quiet as I could in every way. My arm would drop while holding the book, so I started propping the book on a pillow. I tried some affirmations.

"I am worthy?"

It took many, many tries to say that phrase as a declarative statement rather than a question or an apology. In the midst of practicing, I found myself wishing I could attend the hippie church service up on the mountain led by Brother Jessie, a healer I had heard about. I realized I was stopping myself out of simple fear. I resolved to bring my unarmored, timorous self to the church no matter how insecure I felt the very next Sunday.

That morning I dithered over what to wear. Who even was I now? I chose an intricately patterned, long skirt in earthy colors and a shawl. I was a penitent, that's who I was.

At the service I stayed silent, feeling vulnerable. As it ended, the congregants gathered near Brother Jessie. One by one he held them close. *Oh*, I thought, *how I wish* . . . Then the words "I am worthy" floated through my mind. I was the last one in line. Brother Jessie spoke quietly as he held me, saying, "Elisa, you have a deep well of joy within you."

These few words rang true. Suchness, the golden joy of life, was accessible to me once again.

TWENTY-SEVEN

This or Something Better, 1984

In the following months my health improved and work was steady. Gene, the owner of the tiny paint store on the outskirts of Sonoma, badgered me to meet up with a young architect in town. "He's weird, he likes old style stuff like you do," he prodded.

Here was an opening, perhaps a sign. I called the architect, Ned. At his office we talked about historic paint, custom tinting, and the fun of mixing arcane materials and historic paint techniques. He asked me to meet his clients at their winery at eleven the next morning.

"And bring samples of your faux work," he said as I turned to leave.

Samples? Uh-oh. I didn't have any samples and only a vague notion of the decorative painting he described. I had never actually *done* any of it. "Well, tell me what your clients are looking for, Ned, and I'll be sure to bring the right samples tomorrow," I said with a casual tone.

Yikes. On the way back home I stopped at the bookstore and bought the one and only how-to book of specialty finishes they had. I headed to Gene's place for super-fast drying varnish. Back home, I cut some old bead board from the potting shed into equal lengths. It was painted already, which saved me the step of priming. I fired up my blow dryer and began layering coats of custom tinted transparent paint. These samples had to be dry by morning.

Through experimentation, I created finishes that, at least to me, looked like layers of iridescent Thai silk in the colors the clients wanted. I never heard of Thai silk and there was no internet then, so I had to wing it. I prepared a couple of other options too. The meeting, at an estate surrounded by hundreds of acres of grape vines, went smoothly. Everyone raved over the samples, in part because they were on bead board, a humble turn-of-the-century material that happened to be featured in their new "faux historic" farm buildings. Probably what clinched the deal was my solution for stripping an antique four-poster bed.

"Elisa, we need to strip this finish, and so far no one has been able to figure out how to do it. No matter what chemical they use, the paint won't come off," Ned said when he showed me the carved, powdery white, vintage four-poster bed.

After looking closely at the finish I licked my finger and rubbed. A chalky white smudge came off onto my fingertip.

"This is old milk paint, popular before the turn of the century. Chemicals will never work on this. Just use warm water and a scrubby sponge," I said.

I was hired.

Decorative painting requires courage and lots of experimentation. Creativity requires trust, a willingness to wonder, a kind of innocence. Answers don't always come easy. I tell my trainees, "It is okay *not to know*. By letting yourself *not know*, you create the space to ask the essential question: what does this want? Never ask what is wrong. That's the long way around and might never lead to an answer. Instead, ask what is wanted, and then listen."

Physical effort, science, prayer and some luck: this is my sure fire recipe for transformation. Succeeding in this new career became an obsession, an obsession lasting decades. At last everything seemed vibrant, full of promise. Everything, that is, except our living arrangements.

"James, can we have a meeting? We need to decide something. Let's sit for a sec."

We sat on the steps of the sun porch at Dean's house, looking out at the verdant expanse of lawn ringed with mounds of ivy at the base of tall magnolias and redwoods.

"Work is going well, and I have some money saved. The thing is, we can either move to an apartment on our own right now or we can get a new car, but we can't do both."

James took in the view and surveyed the pool in the distance. Just then the wisteria climbing high in the redwoods released a snow of lavender petals in the slight breeze. "Well, what kind of car?" he asked. "This is a pretty good setup for now."

As we reviewed the car options, our conversation reminded me of the day we chose our last name when he was eight. We settled on a boxy SUV and agreed on the color.

"Can I take it to the prom?" he asked.

"Sure, we might even be able to move to our own place by then."

The creative visualization techniques in the self-help books echoed that deal I'd made with God way back on Halloween night in Rescue. Invoke what you want; believe it; bring it to you. I taped a five-year plan for my career, written in the present tense, inside my work binder. A few weeks later, a corporate representative from Benjamin Moore Paints called, referred by Gene. The national rep asked me to develop samples and discuss paint techniques at a three-day conference for architects and builders in a nearby city.

At first, fear held me back. Whenever I finally admit to fear, I try this visualization:

Imagine you stand outside a room; inside the room is the future. Your fear creates a veil; you cannot see into the room. In fact, it may seem the room is filled with fear. But if you allow yourself to commit, to take some steps forward, once you step over the threshold, you have stepped through the veil; you are in the known. The fear is behind you.

I had no formal training as an artist or designer, so it was natural to be anxious. But I'd been invited, right? All I had to do was bring my best work. I got busy and stepped forward into the unknown. My custom samples and energy at the conference gave my career a powerful boost, and again I had Gene, and my own courage, to thank.

The next year, and all the years that followed, the residences I painted with my team expanded in scale and scope. A far cry from the renovated chicken coop at the ashram or the old farmhouse in Rescue, these projects sustained us. The many young artists and painters I trained adapted to my techniques and brought skills to the team I myself did not possess.

The risks and rewards of layering color over color energized me, so much so that James probably suspected me of using drugs again. But the very idea of drugs caused an instant headache, accompanied by a flush of extreme embarrassment and shame. Cocaine was like a steam shovel digging in the same dry hole. How could it have taken me years to realize this?

AFTER THE FIRE:
ONE YEAR

Erick and Claudia invited us for brunch at the Twill House in the late fall. There was much to celebrate. The two of them were featured in a wine country magazine, hailed for their resilience and their art. Grants and commissions sustained them, they were secure, and their bond was strong. Erick was making impressive progress on a new, towering light sculpture, his first large piece since the fires.

The breakfast was rich with meaning, and we toasted the progress they had made. Claudia, a vital, spiritual, German woman, invited us to a "gong bathing" that evening. Her new gong, a three-foot-wide circle of bronze, hung upright, centered in the room. It was clear that this new gong was a strong symbol of recovery for her, and though we didn't know what to expect, we said we would return for the bathing. So far, every experience we shared with our land mates was fulfilling, informative, and thought provoking. We were intrigued.

That evening Claudia gave brief instruction, her accent tender and warm. "Just lie back here, on the carpet, close your eyes, and relax. And so, I will begin." And with that a bell tone gently sounded, then expanded, as tone within tone began an indescribable interplay. She played for half an hour, maybe more, flooding me and Chuck and Erick with intertwining vibrations created by the touch of one soft mallet. Sounds of sorrow, of anger, of tenderness, of delight echoed through and across the wooden room.

Gong bathing was new to my linear husband, and to me. Chuck accepted the experience but did not seem outwardly moved. For me, the variegated vibration was uplifting and seemed to help dissipate some of the heavy judgment I placed on myself after the fire. I felt soothed.

Three weeks later, on the night of the new moon, I invited our neighborhood group, some arty friends, and a local reporter for a dessert party to view Erick's completed light sculpture. He installed the 15' tall piece on the front patio, and that night as people gathered the darkness intensified. The sculpture towered over us and on cue began pulsing color, programmed to look like flames of fire. Within a few minutes, these pulses evolved into colors of springtime. His work astounded the crowd. About thirty people came the first night, and some brought friends the second night. Two neighbors commissioned pieces for their own homes.

There is nothing conventional about Erick. His art is unique. For a couple of years before the fire, Burning Man commissioned pieces, but in many ways Erick was ahead of his time. Now, after losing everything and beginning anew, Erick's vision and dedication were recognized. This sculpture was exhibited at the Sonoma Museum of Art and traveled on to other venues in the coming months.

During the party I overheard a woman comment to Erick, "Make sure you get to keep living here . . ." The rest of her words faded as they walked further away.

The mutually beneficial arrangement was working for all of us. But the agreement Chuck and I offered, the Twill House rent-free for a year, was still my expectation. We had a contract everyone had signed, and I planned to use the Twill House as my writing studio. When my final edit was done, we would offer the space as temporary respite for other artists, like before.

The improvements Erick had made, creating a working studio in the basement, and the care they showed for all aspects of the land gave me pause. How could I nudge them to move on? Were they ready? I would have to say something soon.

TWENTY-EIGHT

Sun and Shadow, 1985

Throughout the 1980s, Grandma Bishop lived in a convalescent home in Sacramento, and during James's teen years, we visited her a few times each year. James played piano in the activity room while I massaged lotion into Grandma's paralyzed left leg and arm, unfurled her clubby hand, and gave her a manicure. We took her and her wheelchair to run errands and then to lunch or dinner.

Grandma never complained about her condition, or even her surroundings. She spent her time tapping out letters to friends and relatives on a small portable typewriter with her good right hand. She used all caps because she could not correct errors using only one hand. She'd say, "Everyone knows what I mean. This is how I do it."

I still have one of her notes, brief and to the point.

CHOOSE YOUR CMOPANY
GIVE OF YOURSELV
DONT SMOKEE

On these visits, her debility was not a topic, nor did we talk religion. We reminisced about Camino, making potato soup, feeding the chickens, and picking blackberries. We recalled summer nights when we slept on beds set up on a platform under the stars and listened to the whisper of the wind in the sugar pines. She never once mentioned Grandpa. I did not mention the scrubbing. We had made peace.

When she was eighty-four and I was thirty-five, I brought Grandma to stay for three days in Sonoma. We went to Jack London State Park, and I pushed her wheelchair over the trail beside the madrone, oak, bay, and redwood trees. That evening after dinner she pointed at the local newspaper spread out on the kitchen table.

"Look here," she said, tap-tapping the tabletop with the index finger of her good hand. "We can make a chicken dinner together." She pointed to the grocery store sales. "The sale is this Thursday."

It was only Tuesday. She knew I planned to take her back in the morning. When I reminded her I had to work, she said, "Well, I've been thinking, maybe I should live here. I can pay you; I have social security."

Telling her no was not enough; her pride and her hope were equally fragile. I needed to be delicate. "Grandma, we have so many stairs here to get into the house, and we live far from the rest of the family. Your visit has been wonderful, but my business takes me away for days at a time, and this is just not practical. I am so sorry."

As I spoke, I put my hand on her good shoulder and gave her a kind of half hug. She put her good right hand on my arm and looked at me solemnly, saying, "Well, the world lost a good nurse when you became an artist."

I accepted this as confirmation that she believed I was an

artist, and also as an oblique apology for calling me a murderer so long ago.

Meanwhile, James continued to work with Valerie, the educational counselor, and his study habits improved. At Valerie's place, in trade for paintwork throughout her house and office, I set up a very small studio in a shed out back where I could make samples. While working there, I invented a logo for my company. I called the design the Hand of God, symbolizing the vibration of color and how it touches the soul. I have used the logo ever since.

While painting Valerie's office, I recounted my Grandma and Grandpa Bishop history. I hadn't shared it with anyone until then. She said, "Gee, Elisa, you're thirty-five. Did you ever wonder why you never told your parents?" Later that afternoon, when I returned to Dean's house beneath the towering redwoods, I dialed Dad's number.

"Hi Dad, it's me. Listen, I have some uncomfortable stuff to tell you. It's not anything bad right now, but something I kept secret . . ."

"Daughter, what the hell are you talking about?" he said gruffly, but I could tell he was curious.

I told him about Grandpa, Wesley, and Brunius, keeping it brief. I didn't say anything about Grandma and the scrubbing.

As I shared "that sex stuff," as Dad later called it, he said, "Okay. Look. Are you planning to sue me or something?"

What? Sue *him*? "No, Dad, I was just wondering why I never told you, that's all."

I hung up. *Sue* him? Geez. A familiar hollow aloneness came over me.

Then I dialed my mother. She now had a doctorate in psychology. I recited the litany, this time including Grandma, the scrubbing, her claims that I was a murderer. Long ago Mom had been a victim of Grandma Bishop's anti-Catholic vitriol too.

My mother listened quietly. After a long pause, she said just three words, "Are you sure?" Her voice was wavery.

Any hope for empathy was dashed. I hung up and walked outside.

I found a circle of sun in the garden and stood beside the blowsy, red roses. The blooms swayed toward me in the breeze. Yet steps away, a shady chill emanated from the darkness beneath the redwoods. Sun and shadow, these persist. This is contrast. This is life.

There had been no purpose in telling my parents after all.

TWENTY-NINE

Redemption, Sonoma, 1987

When I had saved enough money, we moved to a brand new, plain, affordable two-bedroom apartment in Sonoma. Sunshine streamed into the second-story rooms, and we had a view of treetops from the living room balcony. But the tenant agreement came with more rules than I had ever agreed to in my life. Rather than sign a lease, I decided to rent this beige, sterile blank space month-to-month. I was certain this first step would lead to something better. We would make our way now that I was clear-headed, healthy, and financially stable.

At a junk store in Napa, I found six mismatched dining chairs, two funky dressers, and an old trunk for ten dollars apiece. James nicknamed these finds "homeless furniture," but the combination of styles gave our spanking new apartment some energy and wit. I traded painting the interior of a furniture store in town for a sofa, two chairs, and an ottoman upholstered in plain canvas. And James found a black lacquer upright piano with beautiful tone.

It had been years since we'd lived by ourselves, and in this modern, beige-and-white box, we were more clearly defined. No back story; no Dean; no sad escape from death and business failure; no drugs; no secrets. Just us. James was a handsome, warm young man with many true friends, but, while I was healthy and fit, I lacked connections of my own. In that boxy apartment the stark absence of true friends became apparent. Distracted by building my business and reluctant to invite people to Dean's house, for five years I had lived from task to task, busy and isolated.

"James, I wonder why I don't have any friends, besides the people I work with, you know?" I asked one day.

"Mom, all you have to do is let people know you *want* friends. I swear, they're all around you. Just try it, you'll see."

This was a twist. When James was little, he didn't like being told what to do, but he would try something new if he thought it was an experiment—a contest to compare one thing with another. Now he was prompting *me* to take a chance. Whenever fear held me back in business, I forced myself to push through. Maybe the same approach would work with making friends. I called some women from Brother Jessie's crowd, and we started meeting at a dance club every couple of weeks. We called it "Dance Party." This was a start. I was on the lookout for connections, ready to let new people into my life at last.

When I first heard of Curtis Coleman, a custom wood finisher living on the outskirts of Sonoma, I didn't think much about it. But when I heard he worked for clients all over the world, and was considered the best in the United States, I noted an immediate tinge—of envy. This was a sure sign I should check him out.

Tall poplars lined the long, curving driveway separating vineyards and hayfields in the low hills outside of town. As I pulled up to his studio, I came upon a collection of larger-than-life, carved wooden figures set here and there, like giant Renaissance chessmen. Fresh stain was slowly drying as the icons cured in the shade. The gabled, light-filled studio had tall French windows flanked with classic columns, topped with pediments in perfect Palladian proportion and a pair of tall French doors at the entrance.

I knocked, but the high whine of machinery from somewhere inside made knocking ineffective. In the shop I could see a tall, middle-aged man using a compressor to blow dust from a partially repaired, carved wooden camel. Sample panels of rich walnut, oak, maple, and mahogany lined the high walls of the shop, exhibiting the mastery of his woodwork, gilding, staining and waxing. I stepped in.

"Hello? Hello, Curtis. I heard you were the best in the business, so of course I had to stop by," I began, extending my hand. "Hope I'm not interrupting you?"

"Well, even if you are, that's okay. What are *you* all about?" he asked as he bent to click off the compressor. He scanned my painting clothes and glanced at my hand as he stood up, then gave it a shake. His hand was warm, and rough. No doubt he could tell I was also in the trade.

I looked around, and there in the corner of his fantastically outfitted woodshop sat a familiar little spray rig like mine. Laughing, I pointed to the equipment. "I'm a decorative painter and work with paint and color. Hey, I can't believe we use the same sprayer. People tease me about it all the time. They say it's a *girl* sprayer."

"No matter what you call it, this is the best there is when you want low flow. I don't know anybody else who uses one. So, what kind of projects are you doing?"

We talked about my work in San Francisco, marbleizing arched panels in the grand lobby of the historic Bank of America building and wood graining the circular dance studio for Natalia Makarova, a famous ballerina who defected with Mikhail

Baryshnikov. All the while, I studied the carved camel. I could see remnants of old paint still present here and there.

"Hey, Elisa, could you match the color and style of this paintwork once the rest of the restoration is done?" he asked. "This is for Sotheby's, and we have to finish all these carved pieces. We're running a little behind."

"Sure, no problem. If I can do the work here it would be a lot easier than hauling things over to my place," I quickly suggested. Not one half of that camel would fit in my tiny studio behind Valerie's place, and this was a chance to add Sotheby's to my client list.

"Okay. That works. Let me show you around," Curtis said as he held open the door.

We toured the planer and shaper building and circled back to the glassed-in finishing shop. Rather than go back inside, Curtis ducked low through a lattice archway partially concealed by blooming jasmine. I followed. We came to an old wooden building sheltered by a giant spruce. Ivy grew all around. It was charming. It was empty. This simple building soon became my new work studio.

Within eight months, Curtis and his wife, Elizabeth, created a two-story apartment for me and James adjacent to the main woodshop. Our new place, bright and warm, also had giant French windows flanked with fluted pilasters that looked out onto vineyards and rolling hills. I could run for miles on broad country roads, and my confidence in my vision broadened as well. The small studio, twenty steps from our back door, was just separate enough to divide home and work.

Julie, Elizabeth's eighteen-year-old daughter, returned from a modeling job in Europe, and she and James fell in love. Though James had been accepted at Berklee, the renowned college of music in Boston, he chose to remain in California with Julie to study jazz piano and play water polo at the local community college.

This choice was a relief because the few thousand dollars I had saved for James's education would barely cover a summer session in Boston. Certainly, his father, who had been out of the picture for nearly fifteen years, would not contribute. We had not seen him more than three times since we'd lived in Rescue. We heard he had at least three more young children and lived out of state somewhere. I decided long ago not to pursue back child support. Ron claimed he owed nothing because James changed his last name when he was eight. "He's never really been a father to me, anyway, right?" was James' pragmatic conclusion.

The summer James turned eighteen, I was asked to create finishes for a famous designer's line of outdoor furniture. It took weeks to devise formulas that would turn cast aluminum into something believably weighty and precious. The finishes, "pitted nickel" and "ruined gold" transformed the frames of the armchairs, lounges, and settees, making them look more than antique. They looked ancient. James painted the first round of showroom samples, fitting the work around classes, water polo, and the gigs he and Julie had with their band. When the furniture started selling well, James got the contract to reproduce the complex finishes. He rented a giant warehouse, hired help, and set up a practice space for his band there. The expensive furniture was sold to clients like Elton John, Barbara Streisand, Bill Gates, and mavens of the fashion and finance world. James was thriving.

THIRTY

Kismet, 1988

Work was my passion. Still, a companion would have been great if I could find someone to fit into my world. When I turned thirty-eight, I wrote a comprehensive list for "the man I choose to love." As prescribed by Shakti Gawain, these wish lists were to be written in the present tense. The list had worked for my career and for my living arrangements. Why not for a romantic partner?

I wrote, "The man I choose to love is fit, successful, smart, positive, healthy, honest, a good match for me physically and sexually." After pondering, I added "sense of humor" and "available" and realized, with surprise, I'd never dated a man with children. Strange. I added "good father" near the top of the list. "Likes to travel; we go to Hawaii and Colorado."

This ideal man I planned to see once a week, for a few hours. I was too busy for anything more. I taped the list to my bedroom mirror and read it aloud for the next few weeks, adding, "I am worthy," for good measure.

In mid-June, Dad and Marsha invited me to Placerville for the annual Father's Day parade. I hadn't been to downtown

Placerville in more than a decade, and the invitation seemed a kind of olive branch. Marsha and I maintained a polite distance, no matter the circumstances. I knew spending a day in my hometown was unlikely to be emotionally fulfilling, but it was Father's Day. I drove to Placerville.

When we got together, I'm sure Dad could see I was healthier, more filled out. I showed him photographs and major magazine articles featuring my work. "Well, hell, I can't believe you can get these fools to pay good money to make things look old," he said.

"Does that mean you're proud of me, Dad?" I asked with a tinge of sarcasm.

"You could sell ice to Eskimos," he answered as he set the stack of photos down. Dad was not big on praise.

My father drove his restored antique fire truck down Main Street, a key element in the parade, boldly sounding the siren all along the way. His cronies piled on, filling the benches he'd installed where the ladders used to be. I squeezed in to take the ride through town. Marsha, dressed in a clown costume, skipped alongside, throwing penny candy from a big sack to kids lining the street. We made our way through town, slowly passing the row of bars, the dusty hanged man, and all of Main Street. Nothing seemed changed.

After the parade, Dad's current hangers-on gathered around him as usual. When I was approaching to say goodbye, I overheard a man say quietly to another, "Gee, I never knew Joe had a daughter."

At home later that evening, I made a pot of French press coffee and settled in with the paper. Every Sunday, the *San Francisco Chronicle* printed the weekly horoscope. The wisteria, delphinium, jasmine, and foxglove that Elizabeth had planted by my windows warmed in the late afternoon sun, offering up their comforting scents. I found the horoscope. Sipping the dark brew, scanning to the bottom, I saw these words: "Pisces: A new love interest will enter your life this week."

I laughed out loud, imagining everyone born under the sign of Pisces falling in love with someone new in the coming week. Then I seriously considered my options. Where and when could I meet up with this hypothetical love interest? My team was restoring, painting, and gilding an Iranian mogul's mansion in the city, and my commute plus eight hours of work took up most of every day. I didn't drink, so bars were out. San Francisco was also more or less out because there was too much competition. Many men of the right age were already married or were gay, including most of my decorating friends. In the city, it seemed hordes of women were hot on the trail of any available man. So that Monday at five thirty in the evening, I arrived at my fancy gym at the Sonoma Mission Inn and Spa. I even put on a little lip gloss.

In 1988, the Stairmaster was new, a mini escalator. I intended to warm up with forty floors or so and then take a look around. But a tall guy with five-o'clock shadow was already using the one and only Stairmaster in the cardio room.

"You're on my toy," I said to his back. This couldn't be the guy. He was so pale he was blue. In June!

"There's room for two," he countered. I fled to the weight room.

Later, when he wandered by the drinks station, I showed him the iced tea and lemon cucumber water and fixed him a glass, then went out to the pool in search of my ideal man. There were no prospects there. Well, it was only Monday, and my horoscope did say "this week." A few minutes later, the pale guy passed by, then suddenly pivoted and sat down across from me in the circular outdoor hot tub. We were the only ones there.

"Where were you yesterday? I looked for you everywhere," he quipped.

"On a fire truck in a parade. Where were you?" Top that, Blue Dude.

"Racing cars at the track," he said with a grin. Chuck mentioned he was from New Jersey, staying at the hotel while he took a racecar driving class at the raceway outside of town. When I told him about my work, he said he had "been wanting to meet an artist." A few minutes later, he asked me to join him for dinner, but I wasn't hungry. This was not my guy. He was just now figuring out his divorce and concerned about his five-year-old daughter, who happened to be named Lisa. When he suggested dinner again, we were wrinkly from the hot tub. Still not hungry, I invited him to go hiking high in the Mayacamas Mountains ten miles away.

"Okay, then we'll be hungry, and *then* we can have dinner," he said happily.

On the drive, Chuck pulled out a mix tape and turned up the music. Steve Winwood's "Higher Love" was the first song, my favorite. The music, the low sun, and the open convertible all relaxed me; I leaned back in the seat and enjoyed the moment. Then I noticed each of Chuck's four cassette cases had the list of songs, neatly typed, including the artist. Hmmm. In my car, cassettes were tossed around without cases, and I had never made a mix tape in my life. We were way, way different.

High up the mountain, we parked in the midst of thousands of acres of waving prairie grass. Every evening like clockwork, a big wind blew across the range from the Pacific Ocean forty miles away. The day before summer solstice, at seven in the evening, it was still daylight outside. The grasses waved in undulating surges, moved by the gentle but persistent wind.

Thinking of how I ease my mind when anxious about change, I offered Chuck some instruction.

"Look," I said. I stripped some tiny purple blossoms from the wild vetch growing beside the trail and explained, "Eat these flowers, think of your daughter, and imagine the best way things can turn out. Then turn and face the wind, open your arms, and let the breeze move through you. This is how I ask for guidance, and then I usually say, 'Thank you, God.'" As I spoke, I was thinking, if he eats these flowers, maybe he *is* the guy.

"Am I supposed to eat these bugs too?" he countered. On his palm next to the delicate petals crawled a few miniscule black bugs. I had been eating wild vetch in the late spring since I was four and had never once seen a single bug.

"No, not the bugs," I said, laughing.

Chuck ate the tiny violet petals. He turned to the wind and paused, offering his prayer in silence. When he finished, he turned to me, saying, "You know, I think you might be Jewish and not know it."

"Really, why?"

"Because Jews have a blessing for everything."

Then we went to dinner.

It took some negotiating on his part, but once we lay side by side in his hotel suite, I required no more coaxing. For the first time ever, I felt trusting. Open. I wondered out loud how this could be.

"It's simple," he said. "It's kismet."

Kismet—because if we'd met any earlier, Chuck said, we probably wouldn't have liked each other much. I was an artsy moon-dancing chanter who claimed to be free and strong. He was a driven corporate man who loved sex and adventure. Chuck was a celebrated marketing genius, linear and strategic. He was witty and restrained, with a smooth style. I was self-taught, intuitive, and swirly. I had behavioral wrinkles and ridges, markings and scars. Some, left over from cocaine use, were slowly dissipating. Others were embedded in the red dirt of childhood, hidden beneath my flower child wreath.

At dinner the second night, I grasped Chuck's arm. "I know this is going to sound weird, but just this moment I began to see everything in brighter color." He looked at me intently but said nothing. "I think I know what this might be," I continued. "Ten years ago my boyfriend died. It was like a shadow spread over everything. Just now, that shadow went away."

Chuck took my hand but made no comment. We hardly knew one another, and this personal transition might have happened for me, with or without Chuck. After all, it was ten years since Harry died. One thing was certain, the powerful sexual connection and the intriguing differences in our personalities led to strong attachment on my part. For me, the lifting of the darkness intensified everything, including my innate desire to attach.

THIRTY-ONE

Diamonds and Rust, 1989

Chuck became my long-distance almost boyfriend. In Colorado, a couple of months after we met, we hiked blissfully at high elevation, polished all over after hours of reunion sex. As we marched up a steep trail, I shared the story of never seeing or holding my first baby. When I glanced back, I saw tears tracing down Chuck's face as he quietly trudged along behind me. Yes, we were different. But only as different as a red M&M and a yellow M&M; our operating personalities formed this thin bright shell designed to attract attention and at the same time protect our interior selves. When we spent time together our hard candy shells melted away.

On that Colorado afternoon, under a daytime full moon, I knew. Here was my man. In the years that followed, I would struggle because of our differences, because of my fears, because of my intense attachment.

My mother, who had been skeptical about most of the men I dated, liked Chuck. Long ago she said she hoped I would find an "engineer type, someone who thinks you're *fascinating*." Was this her indirect way of saying I was complicated and unpredictable?

She must have hoped a linear thinker would find these traits compelling. To be considered fascinating would be a plus; this was kind of on my list, but my current list left out a couple of things. One: lives nearby. Okay, we were working around that. Two: enjoys fidelity. We spent years seeking to reconcile that.

In 1989, when we had been dating nearly a year, Chuck and I were zipping through New Jersey traffic in his two-seater sports car. Loud riffs of Deep Purple's "Smoke on the Water" trailed behind us. Our dating had become serious enough that Chuck wanted me to meet his daughter, Lisa. At six, how would she feel meeting me for the first time and having to sit on my lap? Just as the car came to a halt, I heard a brisk tapping at my side window. Lisa whipped open the passenger door, swung her book bag down by my feet and scrambled in.

"My dad told me you like rocks. I found this rock on the playground. I think these shiny things might be *diamonds*," she said breathlessly. Lisa leaned against my arm and twirled a black chunk of sparkly asphalt in the sunlight between us. Her head turned this way and that against my chest as she looked for the seat belt buckle. I could smell little girl sweat and dust in her long, golden brown hair. Though she appeared carefree, I noticed her back was stiff, and her tan legs felt a bit rigid. I buckled the belt across the two of us as Chuck navigated the crowded parking lot.

"Wow. Hi, Lisa. You're right. I love rocks. This is so cool! Thanks."

Chuck idled along the school circle behind the lineup of cars and turned down the music. Lisa softened, and I took some slow deep breaths. We rose and fell in a discreet tandem rhythm. Somehow, we were already holding hands. I cradled her as we studied the rock, then both of us instinctively braced ourselves as Chuck reached the street. Revving the engine, he zoomed us toward home.

Later, in the bath, I showed her a game with two wash-cloths, a mommy and a baby swimming all around. She traced my movements, and then looked up. Her dense eyelashes, dotted with giant drops of water, captured the light like Man Ray dew.

"Are you a real artist?" she asked.

"Well, sure. You are too. Anyone who does art and tries to show what they feel by drawing or painting is an artist. We can do some artwork together if you want."

Lisa's paintings of vibrant watery hearts and rainbows covered the refrigerator and some of the walls in Chuck's kitchen. In her room, I had seen notebooks filled with carefully printed pony stories, the pencil pushed so hard to the page the words looked embossed.

She asked me into the bath with her. After considering a moment, I stripped off my clothes and settled in behind her. We turned the hot water to a thin stream, and she slipped around, over and beside me like a soapy, muscular fish. Later, when she stood before me to be toweled off, I saw she had a beauty mark deep in a crease where almost no one would see. Like mine. Even on the same side. After wrapping her hair turban-style, I did the same and lifted her up beside me. We gazed at ourselves in the misty mirror.

I wondered, was she really fine, so very trusting as this? Could it be this simple? Just leap into change like she jumped onto my lap and then away we go into the everlasting unknown? Her willingness to trust seemed like a miracle. Maybe this was what it was like to feel safe. I wondered if I could let myself trust in the future, though not everything I wished for was present in this moment. Chuck deserved some time to air out after his fifteen-year marriage, but how much time?

Marriage had not worked for me. I was certainly no expert on relationships. I decided to take my mother's advice and focus on what Chuck brought into my life, not on what was missing.

Almost every other weekend I flew to New Jersey, and on Saturdays and Sundays we watched movies, flew kites, and made cookies. Lisa and I painted countless pictures on rainy afternoons. The whole year I kept checking to see if Lisa still seemed fine. I checked less and less because, for the most part, she did look like she thought she was fine.

We went for walks in the nearby nature preserve to our secret place, where the twigs of a large bush lay over and made an arching patch of shade. One day, I stopped on the path where tall grass surrounded us to look at a huge purple thistle in bloom. As we studied the big puff of deep violet, we realized the thick stalk below held two giant praying mantises, their color matching the stalk so perfectly we mistook them for twigs. Both of them looked our way, swiveling their flat, triangular heads. Just then a fat, bright yellow bumblebee landed on the center of the puffy thistle; as the bee burrowed, the stalk swayed side to side. Yet the pair of mantes still watched us, undisturbed. They turned their heads, keeping us in sight, as they swung to and fro beneath the fluffy bee.

We were dazed with awe. Wordless twins, we looked back at each other, in a ring of magic; the closer we looked, the more life we found. And because we truly looked, we too were seen. Serenaded by the high hum of June locusts, we trudged back to the house in the late afternoon sun. When we tried to explain our experience to Chuck, we realized that our discovery in that moment was simply too deep for words.

One afternoon not long after our mantis encounter, Lisa and I were in her bedroom folding towels and sheets warm from the dryer.

"Elisa, do you like Mike?" Lisa asked me quietly. Mike was her mother's boyfriend.

"I think he's nice; I don't know him, really. Do you like him?" I answered in a neutral tone.

"Well, but if you did know him, you might really like him, you know? And he would probably really like you too. Maybe if you did really like him, he could be *your* boyfriend," she answered. Lisa leaned against her headboard and traced the stitching on her new comforter. She regarded me quickly with a sideways glance, then looked down again.

"Oh. You mean, maybe if Mike and I were together, then your mom and dad could be together again, like before?"

"Yes, and no one would have to be lonely."

I sat down next to her, looping one arm around her, smoothing her hair, and took a long breath. I was humbled. How could I forget the complicated figuring that had gone on in my own head at her age, trying to make sense of things I could not change? I was grateful she showed her lonely, hopeful self to me. Without any way to answer her, I asked if she was "having some feelings."

"I guess so," she answered, then hopped off the bed and started playing with one of her Breyer horses, trotting it across the bookcase with vigor. I didn't press for more, but from that day forward, "having some feelings" became our code phrase, a careful opening when we wanted to explore something sensitive.

Lisa is thirty-six now, just married, and lives only half an hour from us in Sebastopol, California. Her pony stories came true, and she rides every day. She's probably coming in from the barn right now. I try her cell, hoping to catch her. Before the call, I don't stop to assemble some kind of cover. I just jump in, taking a hint from her leap of trust that first day.

"Lisa," I say when she answers. "I just realized how long it's been since I told you I love you."

THIRTY-TWO

Listening, 1990–1993

Visiting Chuck in New Jersey gave me access to designers on the East Coast, and through my work with the architect Ned in Sonoma I met Mark Hampton, a scion of Manhattan decorating. My first project in Manhattan included wood graining, gilding, and patterning many of the thirty-nine rooms of the former Rockefeller apartment on Park Avenue. When working in New York, I stayed with Chuck. Balancing our careers and staying connected was a challenge, but we managed. He wanted me to be me. To him I was not too much—except when I wanted promises like marriage and forever.

One rainy Saturday in 1990, when I was forty, Chuck and I were listening to music at my house in Sonoma. Across the valley, broad cloud shadows rolled over the vineyard-covered hills; patchy chunks of rain were followed by golden sun. The weather reminded me of Rescue, that rainbow day with Jamey so many years ago. Drowsy and a little bored, I asked Chuck to show me my name in Hebrew. We got some paper and a black pen.

"Let me show you Hebrew cursive first," he said.

As the Hebrew letters emerged, I noticed he was writing right to left.

"Right to left?" I asked.

"Yes, everyone else writes backwards," he said, laughing.

The delicate loops and lines were indecipherable and unfamiliar. I had never seen anything like this before.

"Here's Hebrew in the original form. I'll show you your last name," Chuck said as he turned the paper over and started making stiff, stick-like marks.

As Chuck started on my last name, the S in Stancil looked exactly like my logo! And as the letters continued, I realized *this* was the ancient writing I'd seen in my dreams, on pages of an ancient book when I was just eighteen.

"But Chuck, this is the writing! I saw this writing in my sleep a few months after the baby died. I tried every night to bring the message, the secret of life, into my awareness when I woke up, but the dream turned to mist. And this letter here, look; this letter is like my logo. I call it the Hand of God."

"That's the *shin*. It's used as a hand gesture by Orthodox Jews as part of a blessing." Chuck told me. "For you, maybe it *is* the Hand of God."

On Rosh Hashanah, I went with Chuck and Lisa to temple for the first time. The effort of reading the transliteration and checking it against the Hebrew reminded me of the Latin Mass. But rather than unworthiness and sin, the Jewish service highlighted valor and honor, or so it seemed to me. The Jewish New Year celebrates the "ten days of awe." These high holy days acted like a magnet, drawing me into a world previously unknown.

At dinners with Chuck's extended family, I began to notice that whenever Lisa or her cousins spoke, the whole table quieted, attentive to what the child might say. This sincere respect sharply contrasted with my childhood experiences in Camino and Placerville. What might life have been like if Debby and I had been heard and seen and appreciated?

As I learned more about the Jewish faith and the ethical values integral to the religion, I contemplated converting. The very phrase "ethical values" inspired me to create a pattern language for a restaurant I designed in San Francisco. In fact, I often suggest to clients of every faith that we include personal symbols of shared values when we develop scrolls, patterns, and foliate shapes for their homes.

When Jewish clients heard I was interested in Judaism, they offered secret hacks for holiday recipes like matzo balls. "Just use the box mix, everybody does." Invitations to temple soon followed. But converting had to be more than a repudiation of Catholicism or an emotional desire to belong. How could I be sure my interest in Judaism was not a subconscious effort to promote myself in Chuck's eyes? Once people convert, they are Jewish forever.

"James, what do you think about me converting to Judaism?" I asked one morning.

"Well, maybe Chuck is right. Like he said when you first met, maybe you're Jewish and you don't know it. You love ancient rituals and the prayer to the new moon, all that kind of stuff— you should check it out."

I listened. I studied Hebrew with Lisa. But I was not ready to convert.

When Chuck traveled for business, I sometimes went along. In 1991 he invited me to Europe, my first chance to travel abroad. I arranged a commission to faux marbleize an entry in Neuilly for the French consul general's apartment; this dovetailed with the beginning of Chuck's three-week trip. I packed my art brushes and a French/English dictionary, planning to buy materials as needed. Why worry?

In Paris we had the beautiful apartment to ourselves, and on the first day Chuck bought me an armload of flowers; we ate chocolates and made love surrounded by rose petals. We were deeply delighted with each other, and I half expected him to propose. Later that evening he did make me a ring, twisting the silver and blue foil from a Baci candy wrapper, and slipped it onto the ring finger of my left hand. When I looked at him in question, he said, "Well, someday I *probably might* want to get married." After an hour or so, I put the fragile little ring in an inside pocket of my luggage with some rose petals. From then on I saved a few petals from any roses Chuck gave me.

When he left for his conference in Lucerne, I was surprised to find working in Paris difficult. My easy-breezy plan? Buy the necessary paints using the French/English dictionary. The reality? Arm waving, sketches, and dictionary references did not translate into, "I need slow-drying mediums, what in America are called glazes." Every version of paint or clear medium I purchased dried super fast, the very worst thing for marbleizing. I sent up a prayer; I needed help. Later that day, I came upon a Frenchwoman hand-lettering a sign outside a shop and explained what I needed, again with few words and lots of gestures, but the product she recommended dried even faster. Unable to artfully blend as needed, I kept the colors subtle, but the marbled effect looked weak, not mysterious nor dramatic. I grew anxious.

When my clients returned, they swept into the entry with great anticipation and then ... silence. *Mon Dieu!* My first disappointed clients. *French* disappointed clients. I explained on the fly that I awaited their review so we could add details "to taste." I stayed two more days, making adjustments. On my last night in Paris, pleased with the results, they took me to the famed Les Deux Magots café to celebrate. I ate raw oysters, smiled, and even drank some champagne, though oysters and champagne never appealed to me much.

Later, alone on the train to Florence, I wished I had my worn copy of *Gone with the Wind*. Reading it might dull my regret as it did during boarding school when things failed to go according to plan.

There were no repercussions in the design world, but in my heart I knew my naïve confidence when heading to France, brushes in hand, had not been sufficient. My lack of research prior to the trip, coupled with distraction from my sexy boyfriend, took a toll on my results. "I did not know what I did not know," as they say in business. I was unprepared. Like way back in boarding school, when confronted with difficulty, I lost my mojo.

Alone in Florence for four days, I was soothed by the Italian palette, where frescoes, faux marble, and patterned ceilings galore backfilled the lingering remorse from Paris. When I joined Chuck in Lucerne, we went to the renowned covered Chapel Bridge to choose a music box, a promise he had made the summer we met. Each night in our room in a grand hotel above Lake Lucerne, while Tchaikovsky's "Dance of the Sugar Plum Fairy" played in the background, Chuck gave me a surprise: earrings made of Swiss lace in the shape of butterflies, and a bottle of perfume said to be made of one thousand flowers.

"I can't believe how much I missed you," he said. "I don't know what's happening. I feel about you like I feel about Lisa; I mean, protective. I've never felt like this before."

"I think this means you love me," I responded.

Traveling around Europe was everything I expected, romantic and educational. My provincial Placerville perspective was challenged and expanded. The awe-inspiring gilding and color sophistication of Versailles, the loose, evocative faux marble in Florence, and the precise *trompe l'oeil* of Lucerne were examples of true mastery, gained over centuries. In contrast, much of the American work I had seen—or done myself—now seemed like weak imitation. My confidence was shaken. Like the day I was attacked by the river, my clever Pollyanna perspective failed to prepare me for real life challenges. Humility would be an important addition to my toolbox. I bought used books at a Paris shop and at the Florence flea market with glossy interior images of historic castles and estates. Inspired and intimidated in equal measure, I returned to America.

THIRTY-THREE

Into It,
1994-1999

Back at home, James introduced me to his new girlfriend, Cathy (pronounced cah-*tee*). She was born on Reunion Island, a French province off the coast of Madagascar, and raised in the French Alps. Cathy was of East African, East Indian, and European heritage. This blend created a wondrous combination— cocoa skin and dark eyes—and her French accent made her undeniably compelling. Seeing James and Cathy together reminded me of Chuck's perspective on our differences: "Together we make a whole person."

James likes refined style and fine quality in cars, clothes, and interior design. He has a quick sense of humor and remains as warmhearted as he was as a young boy. Cathy is naturally feminine and graceful, and also practical and structured. English is her second language, so she says sometimes her sense of humor gets "lost in translation."

Her mother raised four children alone, rising to the top of her profession as an educator. Cathy, the only daughter, became the target of her mother's acidic criticism. When we first met, Cathy was a bit careful around me. I see now my brusque, offhand comments sometimes caused affront. My tenderness is not always accessible. Like Cathy's witty humor, my inner warmth can easily get lost in translation.

At just nineteen, after a romantic breakup, she came to America on a whim. A notice posted at a store in Geneva read, "French speaking au pair needed in California." She called the number, and two days later her plane ticket arrived via FedEx. When she brought her two young charges to the Waldorf School in Sonoma, she met James. He volunteered there as a music-appreciation teacher once a week. Julie, in Japan for a three-month modeling job, had suggested she and James switch to an open relationship. So both James and Cathy were suddenly single when they met.

Cathy and James might not have met without the Waldorf School connection, James rarely went into town and spent time working or at college classes an hour away. But soon they became serious. Both wanted to start a family, Cathy sooner than later. "Elisa, what can I say? When I look into his eyes I see my unborn children," she confided. I was in favor of babies, and confess I hoped these future children would have stronger melanin to correct the thin, pink, freckled skin we'd inherited from my father.

When it came time to find a wedding dress, Cathy invited me to shop with her. Significant shopping trips with my own mother came to mind as we headed toward the city, but buying my boarding school uniform or selecting teenage maternity clothes were of a different order. On this day, I hoped Cathy would feel free to explore without fear of being judged.

I promised not to rush; we could go to lunch, maybe even have a glass of wine.

At the first shop, as expected, the walls were lined with voluminous gowns of cream, blush, champagne, every manner of white and off-white, some embroidered, some decorated with crystals, many with lace.

Cathy emerged from the dressing room and, amid the sounds of rustling silk, she stepped onto a riser in front of a three-way mirror. Her everyday demeanor, usually a bit guarded, had been left in the dressing room along with her street clothes. She glowed. Touching the smooth cream fabric at the bodice, hesitating at the embroidery and fine pearls there, then sweeping her hand over the long train in a semicircle, she viewed herself from the side, from the back. Her figure was ideal for the dress: fine shoulders, a very small waist. Her long, wild, mahogany-colored hair and dark umber eyes gleamed in counterbalance to the traditional gown. Turning one more time, she looked my way and confided in her captivating accent, "I would dress like this every day if I could."

Ah, here was a glimpse of her inner self. A fairy princess resided beneath this strong, creative, self-reliant young woman. I hoped Cathy would find me supportive over the coming years, but that day, in the bridal shop, my cautious response sounded kind of tepid and reminded me of my mother. "How will you choose, really? I mean, all of these dresses will look lovely on you."

A year later, in Cathy's village in the Alps, we gathered at the historic Catholic church. The entire interior was painted in complex, breathtaking patterns—on the walls, on every vault and column. Chuck photographed the interlaced, multicolored decoration and these images later inspired patterns James designed in the studio.

My son, now twenty-three, looked European in his fine suit on their wedding day. After the vows and a tender kiss, as they started down the aisle Cathy's wedding dress floated around her like magnolia petals. When she glanced my way, she looked lit from within. At the reception over a hundred and fifty friends and family celebrated vigorously, including my mother and her husband, Jack. Chuck and I bowed out at midnight, unable to keep up with the stalwart French crowd. Most of them joined James and Cathy at a disco and danced until five in the morning.

Soon after the wedding, Chuck became CEO of a start-up on Long Island. I remember now with a cringe the day I invited myself to move there with him. Reading in *Vanity Fair* about cosmetics mogul Georgette Mossbacher and how her bold choices shaped her life, I crafted a self-styled beauty makeover in Chuck's bathroom. I enhanced my eyebrows until they looked like Mossbacher's and put my hair up in a French twist. Then I went to join Chuck as he raked piles of autumn leaves in the chilly New Jersey afternoon.

"I figured out what we should do, Chuck." I said as I handed him a glass of fresh squeezed orange juice. "Since I have so much work in Manhattan, I should just move *with* you, and James and Cathy can have my place in Sonoma."

He glanced with a start at my dramatic makeup, or maybe my declaration, and set the rake aside. "Um, well . . ."

"I can go with you to find the new house; it will be much easier to live in one place, let me tell you. I just read about making brave choices, and this timing is perfect!"

In retrospect, I recall no joyful trumpets sounding. Chuck's reaction was tepid but not outright negative. We had been in a committed relationship for a year already, though that idea *also* was mine alone. My blithe suggestion? "Let's not call it monogamy; that sounds so boring, Chuck. Let's call it fidelity."

In Brightwaters, we found a ninety-year-old French Norman house on the shore of Long Island Sound. It had seven bedrooms, but we could remodel it. Why not?

Though we now lived together, Chuck was not in the marrying mood. "I probably *might* want to get married someday," he said again. Paradoxically, his agreement to try fidelity did not make me feel secure. Deep down I knew he wouldn't naturally choose this. And I couldn't claim to be an expert on lasting marriage or even the benefits of long-term monogamy. My marriages had been very short. Forcing him into a traditional straitjacket—in order to make *me* feel safe—did not make me feel safe at all.

We separated for a few months every few years, frustrated by how well we fit together—in every way, except for this one jagged edge. In Long Island we cooperated on the remodel, and our new master bedroom and fancy bath looked out on the sparkling sound. At Thanksgiving, Chuck's parents and my mother and Jack joined us. I painted the dining room in deep cranberry, from a reference in *World of Interiors*, with faux panelized effects to offset the furniture and rug that once belonged to Chuck's parents. There was subterranean tension in the air, since by now both Chuck's parents and my mother and Jack were perplexed by our lack of wedding plans.

The conventional, stable world of our parents attracted my notice. Could I be conventional? Should I? I filled our house with lovely china and gilt-edged crystal glasses, fancy towels and sheets, custom drapery, all emulating comfort. At the same time, my creative world required risk, the unknown, and solutions that usually involved prayer. I lived divided and distracted.

Chuck's career challenges during this time were extreme. After a year, the start-up appeared doomed. Now he, too, was distracted and preoccupied. The house remodel was done on the inside, but the landscape plan awaited the warm weather of spring. One day I spontaneously suggested we "blow up this picket fence dream" and pack up, put the house on the market and return to California. He agreed. We put everything in storage and moved to a furnished, corporate apartment in Silicon Valley.

Meanwhile, two hours north in Sonoma, Cathy's plan for babies worked like clockwork, and two years after their wedding, she invited me to assist during labor and delivery. I knew her mother would not be in the States, so of course I agreed. But secretly I was nervous. In my experience, birth was fraught with complications. "Stay calm, reassure, and stand by" would be my mantra, but these words could not muffle the tolling bell of loss that rang, sometimes unbidden, in my memory.

"Hi, I am here to be with my daughter-in-law, Cathy Stancil," I told the nurse brusquely as I arrived in the obstetrics ward.

"You can't go in there—only immediate family. You're not her mother." The nurse was working with some papers and did not even look up.

"Well, listen, her own mother is French and is not in the country, and Cathy wants me here. So if you ask Cathy, and she says she wants me in there, then you *will* be letting me in, I imagine."

The nurse grudgingly granted me permission to go into the labor room. "There is no chair for you; the reclining chair is for the father."

Yeah. Okay. No one challenged me when I carted in a small plastic chair from the hall.

Cathy was calm until the contractions got strong. Then she informed us, "You are supposed to be telling me things to do. What are the things I should be doing?" James and I glanced at one another, not certain. I changed the position of the pillow supporting her back; he had her walk a bit; and we tried different breathing patterns. We were supposed to *do something*. All the while, a fizzy numbness enveloped me. During a break, I went back to the nurses' station and briefly explained the death of my first baby and complications of the second baby, asking for more details about fetal monitoring. Would it be hooked up the whole time, and was there anything I needed to know? Reassured, I returned to the birthing room, a bit more present and less afraid.

From the outset, James and Cathy were tender parents. Cathy's gentle focus highlighted a stark contrast between our mothering styles. I believed my baby should feel free, free, free. My job was to keep him safe, appreciate him. Cathy believed in structure and consistency and calmness, probably a better formula for childrearing. James has said, more than once, "I always knew I was loved; I always knew I was protected. But I could have used a little more structure." He would be a good father. And now, at forty-four, it was my turn to be a grandmother—a good grandmother.

All my ideas—what I would do as a grandmother, how I would be—were insubstantial as dust. No plans were needed. Grace notes of wonder and trust rang through my heart to hers and back again the moment I held her. Maeva's arrival was like a tuning fork, organizing so much dissonance from my past into harmony.

We were kindred.

THIRTY-FOUR

Coming Undone and Becoming, 1998-2002

I n 1997, Chuck changed jobs and together we chose a slate-roofed, stone Tudor house replete with diamond leaded windows near the plaza in Kansas City. My plan was to come to Kansas City every eighteen days for three or four days, do job estimating and planning, enjoy time with Chuck, and then fly off to wherever my work was at the time. This was not ideal, but I didn't want to move my business again. I felt no need to penetrate the Midwestern market. Chuck was traveling nearly 80 percent of the time, building a new cell phone company that grew from 500 employees to more than 48,000 in four years.

For the first Rosh Hashanah at the new house, we sat down to the holiday meal, just the two of us. I lit the candles, and after chanting the blessing over the wine, Chuck turned to me and said, with tears in his eyes, "I am sorry. I am not the man you wish I were."

Oh.

The Jewish New Year is a ten-day period sometimes referred to as the ten days of awe, a time for *teshuva*, a time to return to the center of the soul. Some Jews ask loved ones for forgiveness for anything they have done to hurt them the previous year. Some years it's harder to ask for forgiveness, and some years harder to forgive. Still, every year there was much to be learned through forgiveness. This year, as I heard Chuck's words, I realized *I* didn't care for the woman *I* had become. I was not the woman I wished I were. We had begun acting as if all was well, sharing less and less, losing our resonance and joy. Where was my mystical power, my suchness now? This essence lay buried by a landslide of unspoken sentiments and my ongoing pretense that all was fine.

Weary from treating Chuck like a Stretch Armstrong toy, trying to contort him to fit my needs, it was time to switch gears. I didn't ask for any details about his statement; what was the point? It was up to me now to leap over my own internal white picket fence. No more pretense; it was time to get real. I marked everything I wanted shipped to storage in San Francisco, and on impulse invited Cathy to join me on a surfing trip in Mexico. Time to regain my mojo.

Neither of us knew much about surfing, but Los Olas Surf School claimed to make "girls out of women, aged nine to ninety." We qualified. We practiced on big foam boards in a gentle cove beside a village north of Puerto Vallarta. In seven days, I caught only one or two waves. A photo captured me standing barely upright on a fat beginners' board, surfing what appears to be a slight ruffle in the sea. In my mind, I was riding a huge wave.

There's another shot of Cathy floating beside me on her board, smiling in the open ocean, looking carefree. Years later, I learned Cathy's home island, Reunion, in the Indian Ocean, is rife with sharks. Almost no place is safe for swimming, let alone surfing. Cathy had to face serious fears to hang out on the sea for a whole week, though she never mentioned this while we were there. Not long ago she showed me photos from that trip, laughing as she clicked through scenes of blue water. "You might notice I never let my hand or leg dangle in the ocean that entire week!"

Together atop the warm sea we managed to rise above our childhood terrors: her sharks, my aloneness; her critical mother, my accusing grandmother. And we played.

Emboldened, upon return I told friends in San Francisco I was seeking a house for rent. Of course I wrote "the list," and a week later, on a friend's recommendation, I rang the bell of a narrow Victorian house built in 1872 overlooking Golden Gate Park. When the front door opened and I saw the paneled entry and formal living and dining rooms, I was taken aback. This house, with high ceilings and three fireplaces, seemed too nice for *just me*. The master bedroom walls, upholstered in radiant Thai silk, matched the vibrant trumpet vine and bougainvillea blooming in magenta and orange outside the bedroom window. A deck off the sunny kitchen led to a formal garden. The lower floor had a workout room and three-car garage. This treasure of a house was beyond all expectation.

The rent was high but, in truth, something even more concerning worried me. Despite all my business success and many years of affirmations, deep down I did not feel worthy—not *this* worthy. An artist friend I reached out to suggested a trick that worked for her. "Elisa, just envision an embroidered, richly decorated cloak you hold in your hands. This is your 'cloak of receiving.' Swing it over your shoulders and feel it settle over you, and remember, *gratitude* completes the arc of receiving."

As I tuned up my worthiness, I recalled the day fifteen years earlier when I coaxed Chuck to say his first affirmation in Sonoma the evening we met.

"I am blessed beyond my fondest dreams," I cued him, as we looked out over the golden hillside and faced the summer breeze.

"I think it should be, 'I am blessed beyond my *wildest* dreams,'" he said as he raised his eyebrows suggestively.

"Maybe for you," I replied. "But for me, wild dreams can be a lot of work. Fond dreams are more gentle."

Everything about the house was like a dream come true. It was not too much; it was just right. A shady running path traversed six miles through Golden Gate Park, from my front door to the ocean. In this new location, with so many people enjoying the park, running alone felt safe and free. At last I had come to feel worthy—and blessed.

When the owner decided to sell, Chuck surprised me by offering to cosign so I could qualify for a jumbo loan and easily swing the payments. When he came to sign the papers, he was very quiet. In business, he had the nickname "the Sphinx." Chuck was never effusive, and this time he was most subdued. I was grateful but it was clear to both of us that we, as a couple, were no more.

For solace and fresh perspective, I flew across the Atlantic and stayed in London with a friend who was a former client. We shopped for furniture, rugs, and art for my new house. As I neared fifty, this was my first shot at making a home for *me*. My emotions fanned out like one of my paint-color decks: countless variations of bored creams, happy golds, and dramatic darks. I had trouble deciding who—and how—I was from minute to minute. Choosing furniture and art was daunting. I resorted to instinct and got lucky.

At an outdoor stand in Portabella Market, I found a sheaf of original pen-and-ink illustrations for a children's science journal published in the 1950s. The very strength of the inky black strokes, combined with the absolute honesty of untouched white paper, struck me.

In my office even now hangs a framed close-up of an alligator in profile, just his treacherous head, his wily eye alert. You can see into his mouth; his mighty teeth are at the ready. The woman artist's vigorous tenderness, this juxtaposition of energy and emptiness, is the dark and the light of life.

It would be nice to say that childhood accusations of murder, sexual fiddling, lack of understanding, and the absence of protection forged me into a strong and philosophical survivor. There is some evidence this is true. Yet there's the alligator, teeth bared, prepared to tear nearly anything limb from limb.

On an off day, as my trainees and staff well know, I might arrive to the studio or job site in alligator mode, on a vigilant patrol, scouting for a chance to show my teeth and even take a bite. Sometimes I lilt along, blissing out on the sweet air of a spring day, but one frustrating phone call from a job site can drop me—*boom!*—into reptile brain, ready to shred. These tendencies are known, and I try to work around them. Only I know how much I secretly relish these surges of absolute rage. They are like a cleansing, a purge, my own form of scrubbing and bleach.

I warn people that I am primitive. When I'm obstructed, out leaps the mighty gator, but after a few bites, I turn and drag my heavy tail over my downed prey, searching for a sandy shore to sleep it off. Only later do I register regret. Unpredictable and invisible, this uncanny rage is tamped down but smolders. Over time, I have crafted a protective coating. I realize now this coating results in a distance between me and other people—a distance that reminds me of my mother.

THIRTY-FIVE

Seeking Belonging, 1997–2002

I n my late forties and early fifties, when I was single, I trave-led for work, often for months at a time. To complete major projects, like houses more than 40,000 square feet, my team of six or more women artisans often worked six days a week. We needed stamina—and humor. The creative, strategic and physical demands required my full attention. In 2000, when reviewing my taxes, I had to laugh . . . I was making more than I ever dreamed and didn't even have time to realize it.

While working for months in Scottsdale, Arizona, creating historic effects for a massive French chateau, I took an eight-week mindfulness course, hoping to ameliorate mood swings and shed some protective coating. Once back in San Francisco, I continued meditating and made a new list for a loving companion. Why not look for someone like me? At a meditation retreat a few months later, I met Adam, a man humming with emotional energy. He was an architect, lived in Seattle, and was a distance runner. We dated and soon became serious, though James and Cathy were wary of this edgy, nervous guy. Adam's anxiety seemed to mount week by week, and my gestures, intended to soothe, merely escalated his needs. Perhaps kismet put Adam in my path to teach me what insecurity feels like from the other side. Within months the affair flamed out.

Meditation was helpful, but I needed something more. I began working with Richard, a behavioral therapist, and for the next three years we met weekly. While we revisited my past and my actions and reactions to my family and work life, Richard did more than allow me to see myself. He showed me, over time, what it felt like to trust. I have worked with him off and on for twenty years.

In the early phase of therapy, I also began meeting with Rabbi White. I studied Judaism, exploring whether to convert. After a year, I asked the rabbi, "How can I ever be ready? There is so much to learn." He smiled and after a moment, replied in a wry tone, "Elisa, the fact that you realize you will never be done studying supports my theory that you are, indeed, ready."

Conversion as a Conservative Jew includes an interview with three rabbis and the traditional *mikvah*, a ritual bath. Across the street from the Jewish Community Center in San Francisco, Rabbi White ushered me into an office adjacent to the tiled room where the private *mikvah* ceremony would take place. Three rabbis were introduced, and we took our seats. "How did you first become interested in Judaism?" one asked. I told of my hike with Chuck, the wind, the flowers, the prayer. I explained the ancient writing, sharing the secret of life, and how I later learned it was Hebrew.

"What makes Judaism different than other religions, for you?" asked another.

"The respect for children is a big deal for me, but the idea that all we see and all we know emanates an indwelling light, the light of what many call God. . . ." I hesitated a moment. "This I know to be true."

We all sat quietly for a moment. The third rabbi asked, "Is there anything else you would like to share?"

These questions were not about details from the Old Testament or certain holidays; this was not catechism. This was honor, and kindness, and for me a tremendous relief. "Well, look. The primitive beliefs are so compelling, like the prayers to the new moon and the ten days of awe. They seem like the first ideas of how to be human here on the Earth. Is it wrong that the newer aspects of the faith, like Hanukkah, don't move me nearly as much?" I asked.

"No, it is not wrong," Rabbi White answered. They all stood up.

"Elisa, you are a mystic. Come join *my* congregation," the rabbi nearest me said with a warm laugh. Relieved, I left the room to prepare for the ritual bath.

Alone in the dimly lit, tiled room, I immersed myself in the deep, warm water, and recited the *mikvah* prayer in Hebrew. A tender validation spread through me as I repeated the prayer and immersion a second time and then a third time. The tradition helped me relax and feel this rebirth, this renewal, as deeply as possible. Officially welcomed to the ancient tribe, I was now a Jew, and as it is written, I will forever be a Jew. This cannot be undone. My Jewish name is Eliza Chaya, meaning Happy Life.

Some say the Jewish calendar is lunar, not only because the moon marks solstice, but also because the moon is a symbol. Most calendars are based on the sun, but the moon is unique. The moon alone lights the night with the reflected glow of the sun. Like the moon, our souls reflect the indwelling presence of God. The Jewish New Year is a time of pondering the year just passed and the year to come. Jews can ask forgiveness of people they may have transgressed, knowingly or unknowingly. Tradition holds that forgiveness must be granted. This is a reset, a do-over, a cleansing, a healing.

Years would pass before I thought to take this opportunity to ask forgiveness for, and grant forgiveness to, myself.

Margaux, my second granddaughter, was born when I was forty-seven. Long and lanky, she had a powerful cry, and for the first two years belted out her indignity and frustration at unexpected times. James called this her "jihad." When she was old enough to communicate verbally, it became clear she had a great deal on her mind.

"Watch, Grandmama," she said one day before she turned three. On the city sidewalk outside the studio, she walked ahead, very fast for half a block. Turning to face me, she said, "See? That's how strong my brain is."

As soon as the girls were old enough, we went on paddleboat rides in Golden Gate Park, cruising under stone bridges, coasting along to watch turtles sunning on the slopes of the shore. I cycled with vigor to make it all the way to the tall waterfall beside the red Chinese pavilion. All the while Maeva waved her princess wave while Margaux gave instructions.

By the time the girls were four and seven, I began taking each of them on two- or three-day adventures in California. When Margaux was eight, she trekked with me down the trail beside the South Fork of the American River. We toured a string of tiny towns that were part of the Gold Rush history of my childhood.

When the girls got older, we traveled to Vancouver, Manhattan, Lake Shasta and Los Angeles as a prelude to their sixteenth birthday trips, when each girl could choose to go anywhere in the world. I had promised Chuck's daughter, Lisa, the same, and when she turned sixteen we went to Paris for a week, though Chuck and I had not been together for two years.

Chuck called me one winter evening about three months before Lisa's trip.

"What are you and Lisa planning to do in Paris?" he asked. He trusted me to take Lisa alone on her first trip to Europe but was a little cautious. When our week in France was over, he planned to take her on to Israel.

"Well, don't worry, Chuck; at sixteen Lisa just wants to see and be seen, you know? We'll play it by ear."

He reminded me where to catch the train to Versailles and suggested we go to the Eiffel Tower early, on a weekday. He knew I had no sense of direction and difficulty reading maps. I wanted our trip to unfold, not follow a linear plan, but I duly noted his suggestions.

This rite of passage was a gift, a chance to show each girl, at sixteen, that she was valued on her own terms. With Lisa, I would celebrate the wonder of an international city, and together we would experience ourselves within it. When it was her turn, Maeva would choose a summer sailing trip to the Greek Islands; three years later, Margaux asked to trek to Machu Picchu in Peru. For me, this travel was a worldwide do-over. I could re-experience my own sixteenth year in a new way—not pregnant. Not banished. Not Catholic. Not a murderer.

In Paris, Lisa and I stayed in the Marais, the Jewish Quarter. Our building had been built in the seventeenth century, with thick, rustic beams angled so low we almost bumped our heads when we got up each morning. I went on early runs to the Seine, looping around the glass pyramid at the Louvre and returning to the apartment with croissants and fruit. This gave us each some alone time. There had never been hierarchal energy between us; I was not Lisa's mother, nor really her stepmother. We made plans as friends, though she was three decades younger.

The World Cup was in full swing, a big deal in Europe. One morning, on the open metal stairs of the Eiffel Tower, we came across the Scottish soccer team on the stairs above us—in kilts!

They hailed Lisa from high above and bounced a soccer ball down to her. On the night of her actual birthday, we celebrated at a fireside table in a neighborhood restaurant. At the end of the meal, when our waiter learned Lisa's favorite dessert was chocolate mousse, he brought an immense bowl, presented her with a spoon, and gave a bow.

"Take my picture, Elisa," she said as she curled her arm around the giant bowl and held the spoon aloft. "I want to remember this for the rest of my life!"

On our last day, while shopping in the lingerie department of Galleries Lafayette, a harsh buzzer sounded, and a nearby saleswoman gestured me to hurry. In a combination of English and French, she said briskly, "There is a flash sale, Madame! What size brassiere, Madame? What size?"

I dithered, trying to figure out how to say our sizes in French. She leaned over the counter and clutched one of my breasts for a split second and then one of Lisa's. Saying simply, "*D'accord*," she disappeared. In a few minutes, we were presented with finely made bras to try on. They fit us perfectly.

This was Paris.

The day we were to meet Chuck, an airline strike affected all flights from Paris to Heathrow. After some finagling, I was pleased to secure seats on a small plane to London City, which I cavalierly assumed was just another way to say Heathrow. Why worry? When we landed, the little airport outside our plane window was definitely not Heathrow.

We gathered our luggage, and I stood in the small waiting area, my heart pounding. Chuck was undoubtedly at Heathrow looking everywhere for us. What could I do? Just then a ticket agent walked toward us and asked, "Are you Lisa and Elisa by any chance? I have a man on the phone for you." It was Chuck.

I was relieved and impressed that he knew me well enough

to guess where I might be. We took a cab across London, and as we sped to the outskirts of the city to join Chuck, I asked the driver to take a detour so Lisa could catch a glimpse of Buckingham Palace.

Of course, I was still in love with Chuck, and here we were, all together in England. He invited me to stay on and tour the English countryside before the two of them left for Israel.

"I booked two rooms; you can stay with Lisa if you prefer," he said evenly.

"Let's stay together tonight, you and I. I've missed you," I answered.

The next day, the three of us went to Blenheim Castle. As I stood at the massive Georgian entry, I was startled to see giant eyes painted in the panelized ceiling forty feet above us. Rendered in a style reminiscent of Rosicrucian art, eerie single eyes ringed with gilded rays looked down from the center of each panel. The regal blue, bright gold, and fresh green colors had faded and were soot-stained, but this aged effect enhanced their power. The eyes reminded me that there *will* be a day of reckoning. One day we will each dissolve into a never-ending mystical mirror, and we will see all that is, and always has been, simultaneously coming undone and becoming.

We toured the grounds and the castle for hours, and I successfully photographed the mysterious eyes. When Lisa and Chuck traveled on to Israel, I returned home to San Francisco, where I taped pictures of the "eyes of Blenheim" near my computer. Chuck and I were not together, but we had been witnessed, we had been seen. For now, this was enough.

THIRTY-SIX

Roses All Around, 1999

When I was forty-nine and still single, my mother and Jack bought a new house in Roseville, California, half-way between San Francisco and Lake Tahoe. When commuting to big projects in Lake Tahoe, I usually stopped by. One day, Amanda, an outspoken New York artist new to my team, was riding with me. Mom met us at the door. This was the first time I had visited my mother since her therapist had prescribed Prozac. While Mom showed Amanda around, laughter trailed them from room to room. As I munched a toasted tuna sandwich she had set out for our lunch, I pondered Mom's happy mood. In the kitchen, reflections from the pool cast dancing patterns across the ceiling and down the wall, a wavy lightshow. Amanda and Mom rounded the corner and entered the room together.

"You never told me your mom was so funny. She's Gracie Allen all over again!" said Amanda, sending a big smile Mom's way.

Mom? Funny?

"Oh, my God, Mom, do you mean to tell me you have been funny all this time?" I was not joking. I was dead serious. Could I have misjudged her my whole life?

Mom just laughed, sparkly and bright, and set out some cold drinks.

It was as though Amanda had bumped my arm while I was looking through a kaleidoscope. The "mom" pattern shifted and fell into a dazzling new design. My mother was funny! This changed everything. I began calling her on my cell during long commutes. Before long, we were confiding in each other, not about the past but about the present. The more we shared, the less tension remained. She listened with patience to my saga of middle-aged dating.

One weekend they flew in Jack's plane to Scottsdale, where I was working for a few months. We toured the giant job site, a recreation of another chateau, this one included a moat. At my hotel suite that afternoon, we watched *Something About Mary* and laughed so hard we immediately watched it a second time. Later, at my favorite Italian restaurant, handsome waiters flirted with my mother through dinner. The next day she suggested we go back for lunch *and* dinner, since "going anywhere else would just be a waste." Finally, at forty-nine and seventy-six years of age, Mom and I were friends.

One day soon after their visit, I was looking through a magazine while on a flight. The pages fell open to a short article about mothers, daughters, and death. The writer chronicled the ritual washing of her mother's body and, as I read, I hoped someday—in ten or fifteen years—I would be as strong as the author when facing my mother's death.

The following year I noticed my mother having mobility problems, likely caused by Parkinson's disease. She started skimming along beside the back of the couch, transferring her grip to the corner wall by the kitchen, and leaning against the counter as she made her microwave coffee. After a bit of thought, I sent her a short letter asking if I could go with her to her next doctor visit.

Did she think it was time to discuss physical therapy? I expected her to say no, but she welcomed the idea.

Mom's gait and balance were tested, and physical therapy was prescribed. Thinking she felt vulnerable, I spoke up. "Doctor, I don't want to push Mom to do something that isn't comfortable. It's just that she's my best friend, and I want her to last." Amazed to hear these words tumble out freely, I shot a glance toward my mother. Her shy smile and tears were a confirmation. At last, in real time, in front of one another, we each could be ourselves, unguarded, accepted. Mom *was* my best friend.

This was a miracle.

Late that afternoon, we walked arm in arm to her mailbox. Her cane, prescribed by the doctor, was looped over her arm like a purse. When I laughed, pointing out that might not be what the doctor had in mind, she said, "Oh yes, I have it here in case I need it," sounding very much like Gracie Allen.

As we headed back toward the house, she stopped and turned to me, her hand on my arm. "You know, Elisa, I really like Chuck. I have a feeling you'll still end up together."

"Really, Mom?"

"Yes, I see you with Chuck in the end."

A family trip was planned to Lake Tahoe the very next week, but instead, everyone gathered at Mom's bedside in the hospital in Roseville. She had suffered a massive stroke. When we learned it was hopeless, James and Cathy brought the girls to say good-bye. I asked Cathy to bring some roses.

The little girls marched down the hospital hall, carrying so many roses their faces were almost obscured. There were red roses at every stage: prim, tight buds; blowsy and florid; and some perfect, half-opened blooms. Cathy whispered that they'd had a hard time finding fresh roses late in the afternoon on the two-hour drive to the hospital. At the last place they stopped, the florist gave her these at no charge. They were perfect.

When we entered Mom's room, Cathy arranged the flowers in two water pitchers. Mom remained unconscious but appeared to be quietly sleeping now that the breathing tube and IVs had been removed.

With Margaux on my hip and Maeva clasping my hand, we approached my mother's bed. Margaux, a year and a half old, began a series of slow, solemn pats to my back. Maeva, four, put her hand on Mom's bed and softly stroked the sheet.

"Thank you for bringing these roses for Great-Grandmama Joan," I said. "Her mother's name was Rose, so your flowers will keep her company, just like her mother is with her."

They nodded without saying a word. The humming fluorescent lights matched the internal, high-frequency alarm echoing in my every cell. My mother was dying. There was nothing anyone could do. James and his family continued on to the vacation house in Lake Tahoe. I hoped to join them before the week was over.

My brothers and Jack were in a nearby waiting room. "Letting her go," as the nurses called it, meant standing by while Mom's lungs slowly filled with fluid that would, in a few days, deprive her of oxygen. I put lotion on my mother's face and lip balm on her lips, sang a little, and then relented, just in case she really *could* hear. Mom remained still and stirred restlessly only if my younger brother, Ed, came in the room. She was always most connected to Ed.

On the fourth day, after meditating and taking a quick shower over at Mom and Jack's place, I returned to the hospital. Jiggs stood alone in her hospital room, looking anxious and kind of angry.

"Look, she's just lingering here. Why let her hang on like

this?" he asked as tears began to fill his eyes. "What if we just lower the bed down and get it over with?"

"Okay, maybe we should try it." It would be easier to be done, to end the gurgling sound of Mom trying to breathe. Her every breath was now a wet choking.

"Well, *I* can't do it," Jiggs said as he rubbed his eyes. Jiggs, the sharp-shooter, the snake skinner, and the would-be militiaman—was he really asking *me* to lower the bed? I briefly weighed the idea of sin against the struggle Mom was having and then pushed the lever, slowly lowering the bed to lay her flat, expecting a movie-like ending. In five short breaths she would die. Instead, a mist of spittle wetted her face, and the gurgling sound continued. Just then, Jack pulled aside the curtain and looked at Mom.

"Is this what you want?" he asked bluntly as he waved his arm over her struggling there.

"No," I said.

"Well, I don't either."

I raised the bed again, looked at Jiggs, and went back to waiting. I don't think it would have been murder to help her. It just didn't work.

Beside her bed in the twilight, I pondered how to say goodbye with as few regrets as possible. For her. For me. Soon it would be time. I dialed the mortician from the pay phone in the hall, saying, "Listen. Let me explain what I hope you can do. I need to hear you say you will cremate my mother just as you find her when you pick her up, I mean, with the sheet around her, and the rose petals next to her skin. I just need to hear you tell me this is how you will do it." The mortician kindly repeated the instructions verbatim. I didn't know the actual rules about cremation; I only know what I needed to believe.

I lay down on the cot beside Mom's bed and awakened with

a start at four in the morning. The room was totally silent. She was gone.

I moved the sheet aside but left her covered above the knees and below the waist, respectful of her lifelong modesty. I rinsed her pale chest, arms, and legs with warm water scented with a few drops of oil from a small vial labeled "Peace and Calming." The tiny bottle reminded me of those the miners used down by the river to hold their flakes of gold.

My mother looked smooth, untroubled, unexpectedly luminous and beautiful. Tugging deep red petals from each bloom, I gently let them fall from my hand and watched them flutter and land softly around her face, across her chest, her arms, and down the length of her. I quietly spoke the names of our family women as the petals settled: Cathy, Maeva, Margaux, Elisa, my mother's seven sisters, and finally, my mother's mother, Rose. My mother's skin was still warm. I kissed her goodbye on her forehead and closed the white sheet over and all around her.

Robert De Niro has a pivotal scene in *The Deerhunter*, in the rocky, cold woods. "This is this," he says. I quote him from time to time. Some people don't get the reference or grasp the meaning of what De Niro's character is saying, but when it's all stripped away, this is what we have. This essence, this moment contains all that has been. And in this moment is held all that is yet to come.

The night after Mom died, as I drove to Lake Tahoe, my eyes felt like those in the weird 1960s Keane paintings of mournful children with haunting eyes staring out at the world. Motherless children. I never liked those paintings. Breathing in the night air, I breathed out and let the images go. Just then I noticed the full moon's reflection traveling along in the lake water beside me, keeping me company, a glow floating just ahead as I drove beside the shore to join James and his family.

This is this.

Two months after Mom's memorial, I got a phone call from Tommy, my maybe boyfriend from so long ago, Tommy from the river. I noticed he spoke with a bit of an accent. I heard a lilt in his voice, soft and friendly.

"I live near you on the Peninsula," he said. "I saw your mother's obituary. I wonder if you would like to get together? After my father died, I moved back here from Ireland with my wife and four children. We live about an hour away."

"Of course, I would love to get together. Can you come on Saturday? I'll make lunch for everyone if you like."

Nearly thirty-five years had passed. On Saturday, I lit a fire in the woodstove in the kitchen and another in the formal dining room. A large pot of homemade soup was steaming on the Wedgewood stove, in case Tommy brought his wife and kids. Flowers graced the table.

I heard a tread on the step. The bell rang.

I opened the door to a middle-aged man, part Tommy and part Karl. He was alone. No longer svelte and golden, he was gray and weighty. I wondered what he saw when he looked at me.

We tried the soup. At last I learned where Tommy and Karl had gone when I was fifteen, right after Ivan waved his gun at my mother and Karl, disrupting their plans to secure her divorce in Reno. Tommy said they'd left within days for Ireland, where he went to school and later learned the trade of stonecutting. In the short hour we spent together, we each showed portfolios of our work—his stonecutting, perfected over decades in Ireland; my gilding, wood graining, and complex finishes featured in *Architectural Digest*, *Town and Country*, and *Elle Décor* magazines.

We sipped espresso on the deck, gazing across my backyard, where symmetrical topiary was bordered by herringbone brick and shaded by a pair of palms. Like long ago, we were mostly quiet. I noticed the arched rose arbor, clipped back in the fall, was beginning to bud after the long winter stasis. Our conversation slowed. We had little more to say. Standing tall before he left, Tommy looked toward me and reached out his hand.

"Weren't we just like seals, slipping through the water, those summers on the river?"

These simple words, in his lilting accent, felt like a blessing, deeper than a kiss.

THIRTY-SEVEN

Together,
2001-2005

few months after Mom died, I gathered the courage to call Chuck. In my yellow kitchen in San Francisco, I stood facing the wall, listening to the ringing of the phone. He was not expecting to hear from me. Tenderness radiated all through me at the sound of his voice. Here he was. But what would we say? Who were we now? I told him about Mom, the roses, the lake, the moon. He listened. I asked him if he would like to see me. He said, "Yes, definitely yes."

We agreed to meet in Half Moon Bay on the California coast for a hiking weekend. When we met up, he looked all new somehow, as though a stronger outline defined him. We were cautious, tempered by a tenuous respect for one another's perspective. I'd learned what it was like to be hounded by someone's insecurity when I dated Adam. Chuck was humbled too; he had met a woman he liked, but she was too busy to make room for him on a reliable schedule. We had both been lonely.

On the hiking trail, I walked ahead and wondered aloud what it had been like for him when he was very young. No one noticed that Chuck was visually impaired until he was almost twelve.

Without correction he was—and still is—legally blind. As we trekked along I asked, "Do you consider this a sort of benign neglect? You know, that you couldn't see faces or read emotions all your childhood years? Maybe this makes it harder for you to connect deeply."

When he didn't answer, I turned and saw tears in his eyes.

"Maybe," was all he said.

Chuck was now president of the cell company headquartered in Kansas City. Lisa was about to graduate from a horsey college in Ohio with a degree in business and equine management. He said he was thinking of retiring at fifty, buying land with pastures for horses, next to great riding trails. In California. With me. He also told me, without fanfare, that he started a college fund for both granddaughters while we were estranged. This was my man.

We started looking at property in Santa Barbara, Los Olivos, San Luis Obispo. As we traveled up the coast, we agreed our three-plus years apart had been worth it. Familiarity now seasoned everything we did with unexpected delight. It was a tremendous relief to be *known*.

Chuck surprised me by suggesting we make one of my lists, done his style, in descending level of importance, as we searched for our ideal land.

Land adjoining trails for hiking and riding
Beautiful acres
Good for horses
Creek or river
Road, water, electricity already in
Buildable or with a house

The land we found was in the small town of Glen Ellen, ten minutes from Sonoma, where James and his family lived. Chuck is a negotiating wizard, but the owner required full price, no strings attached. I prayed Chuck would agree to this, and James took a photo of me praying in the meadow with both arms raised to the sky. Chuck paid.

This land was once part of Jack London's Beauty Ranch. Before that, General Vallejo's enormous Spanish land grant included this little corner. Before that it was where Pomos and Miwoks summered, grinding acorns and shaping flint beside the spring fed creek.

As the sky lightens, shadows assemble beneath giant oaks, and sunlight glides across the hillside. Dry yellow grass glows with an unexpected rosy blush for a moment, before settling into being just plain straw. Ten miles away, across the Valley of the Moon, low mountains emerge from a layer of fog. Distant patches of gold and green—patterns of meadow, oak, and vineyard—match in scale the collections of moss and lichen on crusty tree trunks and rocks nearby. Dozens of wild turkeys scuffle about in the pasture where Chuck's horses graze. As the sun warms the hillside, the breeze carries everywhere the tender scent of lavender.

Home. When he first bought this land we drove up from the city, fully intending to carry logs, remove thistles, or clear the pasture of rocks. But most often I spread a quilt in the spring grass and simply drowsed my time away. Nature's renewing sameness mesmerized me, much as Chuck's consistency and his evenness of temper had when we first met.

One rainy weekend, Margaux, then six, stayed with us in the Twill House in the middle of the meadow and helped construct an accurate scale model of the new house design. On the interior of the miniature great room walls we painted—to scale—our future stone fireplace, my piano, and the long library bookcase

I had built for my San Francisco studio. The bookcase was designed to eventually move to a future dream house, though I'd had no idea when or where that would be. Now that day was near.

Our flimsy house model, made in quarter-inch scale, wasn't perfect. Chuck's octagonal office tower was rickety, and the roofs were just pieces of thick brown paper. I hadn't figured out details of the roof design and asking the question, "What does the house want?" brought a range of answers. In building, uncertainty causes delay. Delay is expensive.

A series of deep retaining walls were in place, holding back the hill. Walls were framed and hoisted into position, twenty-six feet high in the front, eighteen feet high in the back. We had committed to a shed roof, but what size and type of beam would support the roof? How far should the overhang extend in the front and back? I called my friend Ned, the architect I had met in 1986 when he gave me my very first decorative painting job.

Sitting on the concrete footing beside the framed walls in the summer sun, Ned used a lumber pencil to sketch ideas on a scrap of wood. He gave us a story for our roof, resolving the intersections of wall, ceiling, beam, and overhang. With this organizing principle, the house came together.

The design accommodated our impending mortality: step-in showers, broad doorways, smooth transitions from inside to outdoors, an extra room for future live-in help. These details made us feel safe, all the while appreciative that none were yet needed. And the seasons passed.

There is no real insurance against dying; no plan can eliminate loss. I know this. My first child's death, my own near death, my fiancé's fatal accident, my mother's and later my father's deaths. Each felt alarmingly unique, yet not one was uncommon. This is this. We live, and then we die.

A rushing creek bordered by towering redwoods marks the

boundary of our land. It is here each year on Yom Kippur we spread a velvet quilt over the soft redwood duff in the center of a circle of redwoods and laze through the long day of fasting. This is our temple. Each year when we rest beneath the lacy boughs, I become acutely aware that life is uncertain. And yet any hour of any day I somehow forget this truth with ease.

Each year, beside the creek, we attune ourselves, searching the filtered sunlight for portents, for signifiers. Squirrels leap and cleave to branches; leaping again, they disappear. A butterfly flutters nearby, then inscribes two perfect circles just inches above us before flying high and away. Will we be granted another year?

On our kitchen windowsill, heart-shaped stones from all over the world are tilted up against the glass, my witnesses and my proof. Collections begin innocently enough, without much thought of ending. And so it is that a huge wooden bowl in the pantry overflows with quartzite, limestone, and serpentine. Tiny heart-shaped shells rest in a tray beside my bed. Despite every certainty of ending, I continue to gather these totems, signifiers of magical realism. Why, you may wonder. Because they turn up whenever I think to look, in Peru or Greece, on a beach or a desert, and remind me that now is the time to celebrate the profound gift of life.

One day our family will choose from these remnants, then leave the remainder with our ashes—beside the creek, beneath the redwoods, where we forgave and were forgiven as we lazed on sacred days and dreamed of past and future.

THIRTY-EIGHT

Just Plain True, 2008

Debby called not long after Chuck and I moved into our completed house on Sonoma Mountain. My heroic cousin needed me in Placerville: her mother, my aunt Betty, was close to the end. I was in a swirl as I packed to leave. Anxiety messed with my sequential thinking. I put one shoe in my bag, one lipstick, my sunglasses, the other shoe. At the last moment, outside my bedroom, I spied five muscular, vibrant lilies nodding in the breeze, psychedelic in their intensity. I added lemon verbena, lavender, and sweet basil to the bouquet, and during the two-hour drive, the scent was soothing. I hoped to bring strength and calm to Betty, who had been ill with pancreatic cancer for nearly a year. We had seldom seen one another in the forty years since I had left Placerville, and now this visit with my aunt might be my last.

Betty, wearing slippers and a thin nightgown, sat at the foot of her bed. Except for her eyebrows, carefully sketched on, she wore no makeup at all. Though her hair was now patchy and fine, she wore no scarf, no wig or hat. The hospice caregiver stood beside her as Betty sewed stitch after stitch; the hem of her nightgown had come undone.

"Hello, dear, how are you?" she asked when she looked up.

I was struck by how real she looked.

Not a vulnerable and frail kind of real.

Just plain true.

Betty endured terminal pancreatic cancer mostly without comment. Debby said she sometimes suggested an over-the-counter remedy as though her symptoms might easily be resolved. On this day she welcomed my flowers and herbs with a smile and declared them lovely. She remarked upon the delightful scent. This was Betty.

We sat together in the living room, in matching armchairs, where the decor appeared unchanged since my childhood. Betty studied the newspaper obituary of a lifelong family friend as her fancy clock on the wall nearby clicked off seconds and minutes. After trimming the article, she carried the two pages slowly to the kitchen and pinned them to her bulletin board. Seeing her scissors move even and sure and the tacks pressed just so into the cork, I thought of the dress Betty helped me sew when I was thirteen.

When I was growing up, Betty was movie-star beautiful. During the summers, riding in Uncle Ken's sleek wooden ski boat across Lake Tahoe, she looked like a model from a magazine. Her soft caramel hair never seemed messy, her skin was flawless, and I could tell she knew she was pretty. When she wanted to make a point, she fluttered her eyelids, but it was kind of weird because Betty had no eyelashes or eyebrows. When she was a young girl a raging case of poison oak, in her lungs and all over her body, left her with no facial hair. She had always drawn on her eyebrows. Yet Betty managed an undisturbed patina of loveliness at all times, so unlike my own mother. When I was little, I thought this reliable sameness was plastic coated. I wondered what was under Aunt Betty's skin, on the inside.

I studied her intently when she drove her big station wagon with us kids piled in back. She knew every word to every song on the radio, but her favorite was "Silver Threads and Golden Needles." She sang loudest when it came to the part about being trapped in a cage.

Was she really happy? Is anyone? Was I?

Remember my scientific study when I was eight, when I tracked my findings about happiness in a notebook for a couple of weeks? Back then I had to let it go. Happiness seemed too elusive to be scrutinized and measured. But the question remained unresolved.

If I discovered Betty's comfort with herself and her world was somehow manufactured, then maybe I, too, could create my own luster of happiness someday. If not, would the dark anxiety weighing upon my own mother be my fate?

Not long after all that pondering, Betty offered to help me sew a dress for my eighth-grade dance. In the fabric store, I hardly reviewed the fabrics. I feigned confidence as I blithely chose a soft blue cotton and an easy pattern and hoped my pretense of casual ennui would stand in for the innate fashion sense I lacked. Betty questioned both the style and the fabric but left the decisions up to me.

Sewing is structured and absolute: facing the material good side to good side; cutting with care; feeding the fabric smoothly under the needle to make a perfect seam. Each step is ordered and precise, each step builds on the success of the previous step. Soon Betty's instructions seemed secretly laden with clues about woman-ness, femininity, and patience. Though her manner remained consistent and optimistic, I feared she might see I had no idea how to be a girl, much less a woman.

What was I doing, trying to sew something with my aunt, a woman so comfortable with herself she was seamless? Stitch by stitch we finished the sleeveless, full length A-line dress. As I tried it on, I saw my wan, unpolished self in her mirror. No dress could offset what I saw as my many flaws: freckles, cowlicky brown hair, and at best a girl next-door attractiveness. True loveliness eluded me. I flushed hot with shame when I glimpsed myself in the mirror. In that brief unguarded moment I saw how much I resembled my own mother.

I wore the dress only one time.

I began to wonder if it were possible for any girl or any woman to be free. Free from unspoken rules demarking acceptable, modulated behavior; free from attack from brothers or men; free to speak and act powerfully, untethered by self-doubt; free to be respected as an individual. Just free. Though I believed I was a person who happened to be a girl, in my town people viewed both me and Debby *only* as girls. It was stifling to have our personhood diluted out of hand.

Now, so many decades later, Betty folded her hands in her lap and asked me to please write her "article," her code word for obituary.

"Nothing too showy," she said.

Ah. This was why she had asked to see me. Betty knew I had written articles for magazines more than thirty years ago. I didn't write my own mother's obituary. Jiggs did, and included things long forgotten—Mom's work with the League of Women Voters, her role in the California Mental Health Commission. Until I read it, I didn't know my mother's hospital ship had been sunk in the Mediterranean during World War II, knew nothing of the valor of the crew and staff who saved the patients, including German prisoners of war. My brother did a better job than I could have.

Aunt Betty repeated her request. "Nothing too showy, dear, I don't want to sound ostentatious. The hospice people said I should think about my legacy. Of course my children are my legacy, but I don't want to burden them with that."

On this day, sitting beside me in her matching easy chair, recalling her life, Aunt Betty didn't mention the deaths of her father, her stepbrother, or her youngest sister when she was still a young child. Stories of the family's poverty and hardships in the town of Camino I learned from my father. Grandma Bishop dressed her four children in black and, as a "poor widow," visited the lumber mill and hardware store, requesting donations of materials to fix up the abandoned schoolhouse. Betty never mentioned living in a tent for nearly a year, even in the snow, while the old schoolhouse was repaired and improved.

At sixteen Betty escaped from Grandma's religious fervor, remaking her girlhood into a chapter in a life where everything was lovely. Dad remarked, more than once, "Well, Betty lives in her own world." In Betty's world, taking sincere care of her husband and family was far more compelling than her distant past.

The wall clock chimed on the hour and on the half hour as we settled on the final details of her article. Time was getting short. I decided to speak up.

"Betty, when I was little, I used to study you. Your house always felt so calm, so different from my house. I used to wonder if it could be real. I felt like I was on the outside, looking in."

I hesitated, not wanting to flat-out betray my own mother or reveal I doubted Betty's happiness back then. In fact, after half a century, my own life was turning out to *be* lovely in many ways. Especially when I let myself just feel it.

"I want to thank you, Betty, I feel honored you let me see you and spend time with you, especially now."

She turned toward me and smoothed her mended nightgown. "You always meant a great deal to me, dear. All the children, but especially you."

She knew it had taken a long time for me to learn to sit still, to let myself hear these simple words from someone in my past.

Debby and I went to the Chapel of the Pines to set things up for the funeral. Her two brothers had selected an urn that looked remarkably like a bullet casing. We exchanged it for a graceful vase etched with delicate intertwining vines. Lovely. While we looked over the chapel's choice of poems for Betty's memorial card, we kept coming back to that ridiculous urn her brothers had chosen.

"Boys." Debby said it flat and plain, shorthand for so much in our past. While we waited for the funeral director, we kept remembering things our brothers had broken up or killed. Debby and I were not the only ones in our families who suffered. Aloneness was a family virus. I can't imagine living with the memories of past cruelties that both my brother Jiggs and my cousin Craig created for themselves.

Debby finished filling out the funeral papers; we chose her mother's flowers and crosschecked that the correct urn would be used.

We were the women now.

THIRTY-NINE

Gather Round the Roses, 2009

n the spring, a week after Mother's Day, my four closest women friends joined me for an outdoor brunch. Cathy brought a vase of heirloom roses for the table.

In business there is a maxim I mentioned earlier: "You don't know what you don't know." When I was twelve I wondered what kind of woman I would become. This seemed as unknowable as the depth of the dark stretch of river in the canyon long ago. On this day, as we took our places, I realized becoming is a lifelong process.

Cathy's photographs reveal her deep, abiding empathy. With her camera she captures the unspoken. Lisa, as young girl, showed me what it's like to feel safe enough to trust and she still takes leaps into the unknown with confidence. Maeva and Margaux are young women now, and their esteem for life, for the family, and for me is a healing grace note, a tolling bell not of loss but of belonging.

After brunch Maeva brought the vase inside, and for the longest time the fragile white roses didn't fade and droop. By the time they began to wilt, Chuck's mother, Renée, was due for a visit.

I prepared the house, tossing the wilting flowers into the compost bucket beneath the sink. A few petals spilled over the edge. Seeing them there I paused, curious. Something about the pattern was familiar, but I moved on, no time to waste. Rinsing the sudsy vase, I saw it was the bottom half of a carafe my mother gave me decades earlier, long before we were friends. Without warning, a wave of time-lapse grief surged up and crested, washing over and through me before dissolving like mist.

My mother . . .

Years before, when we were civil and distant, my mother and Jack came to the first "Celebration of Life" gathering at my studio in Sonoma. James, at nineteen, invited everyone from what he calls our "golden circle"—clients, teachers, art and architecture friends, family, anyone who resonated with the light of life. We rented a big a tent, set up a dance floor, hired a blues band, and prepared what I called a peasant banquet. Rich, hearty food. James nicknamed my mushroom soup, spiced with nutmeg and sherry, "the nectar of the gods." Chuck's parents came out from Ohio.

On that night in 1990, stressed with hostess duties, I sighed when Mom and Jack walked through the door carrying a fancily wrapped present. I quickly removed the silver paper and ribbon and inspected the conventional, two-piece, glass carafe and top, flowers etched on one side. Wary of my critical reaction, Mom suggested, "Um, you can use it for water upstairs by your bed; you see, the top serves as a drinking cup."

Was she saying my artsy house—with no bathroom upstairs—was not good enough? That I was not good enough? Mom's gift *was* handy, until the cup toppled off the nightstand and broke during a mighty night of passion with Chuck. For nearly thirty years, the topless carafe served as a vase, moving from house to house, changing hands, returning to me. The prior Valentine's Day, I had filled it with sprigs of daphne and brought it to Cathy.

The morning of our brunch, Cathy and her girls returned it, filled with the antique roses that bloomed beside their front gate.

Reaching under the sink to gather the withered petals, once again I hesitated, pondering the scattered pattern. But Renée would soon arrive, so I discarded them, moving on with my preparations.

Chuck's mother, moderate and stylish, keeps a clean, almost sterile house. This in itself was not so threatening, but after years of intermittently dating her son, which she graciously tolerated, I was now—finally—her daughter-in-law. We were different in temperament and certainly in housekeeping style.

A bit manic, I touched up the paint, organized the haphazard pantry and tea cabinet, even revarnished the wide plank floors in the great room and kitchen. I worried she might think me messy, reckless, too much, too little. Renée prized gentility to the bone. I still cringe when I recall her wince when I loudly hailed her across a marble hotel lobby many years ago. My natural exuberance, at least on that day, had been out of place. Maybe a well-maintained, orderly house would reassure her.

Together we prepared her special recipe for gazpacho, discussing distant family. Watching her cut tiny squares of cucumber just so, I was intrigued. "Renée, you are so measured. I don't seem to have a moderate setting on my dial. How do you do it?"

"I've always been this way," she replied.

Her short, silver pageboy *is* always in place. Pilates and stretching keep her flexible and trim, though she is over ninety. Perched on our leather sofa, her legs tucked beside her, from a distance she could be mistaken for a teenage girl. In the afternoon, enjoying views of vineyards and mountains, she relaxed outside on the patio beside the hillside of lavender. We collected some and dried it in the sun for her to take home. After a family dinner, James played the piano and Renée beat me at Scrabble.

One morning Chuck took his mother on a brisk ATV ride to the barn to feed the horses. On the last day, she rode horses with him a mile up the mountain.

After Renée left, I coasted barefoot across my shiny floor, lighthearted. Different did not have to mean dangerous. It was okay to be different. Just then I noticed on the front table by the window the Mother's Day card from Cathy, her close-up photo of one pink rose. I recalled those white rose petals scattered all around.

Suddenly, I understood.

On my hands and knees, I looked under the sink and found half a dried petal on the rim of the compost bucket and two fragile fragments beside the dish soap. I held the remnants, thankful for my casual housekeeping style. The dried petals had no scent, they weighed no more than tears. These were Cathy's roses. *Family roses.* I opened the antique painted box my son gave me long ago and let the dried bits fall, watching them land upon the dark red petals inside, petals I saved from the day my mother died. As I closed the box, I saw my mother again, luminous and still, her roses in a pattern, all around.

I saw she loved me.

FORTY

Glen Ellen,
2009–Present

When at last we decided to marry, I suggested we take a road trip to Death Valley for our last "single" Valentine's Day. Rather than the desert in bloom, we encountered a sandstorm that pitted the windshield and paint on my brand-new car. After the storm subsided, we spent the next four days exploring the unique landscape of the desert, an alternate reality.

For days we hiked through canyons and up dry washes, marching to our separate iPod beats, unplugging from time to time to compare notes. Mostly, we just gestured and poked each other, agreeing some stupendous natural form up ahead was "pretty."

I watched Chuck's shadow as he handily traversed a big flat rock, his head bobbing to the blues. I've studied him from every angle, searching for fissures in his façade. He has never liked this. Using my female sonar, I conduct soundings at depth, chart my findings, and generate comparisons. Now it's second nature, and though I could drift free like a tumbleweed, mentally cartwheeling over the immense desert, instead I trudge along, connecting

241

some dots from earlier conversations, wondering if he is happy to be here. I take some breaths and consciously breathe away my anxiety. He loves me. He is ready to marry. He has said so, and this I know: Chuck is an honest man.

During lunch we sat adjacent and fished around for something to say. Damn, I thought this would never happen! For the longest time everything between us glinted with the knife-edge of newness, every moment cut both ways. Now here he is, up close 24-7, while I tap and clatter around his perimeter blindly wielding the white cane of familiarity.

Chuck *is* legally blind without his glasses. Twelve years of childhood without corrective lenses explains his marginal facial recognition skills and accounts in part for his alarming independence. When he sees with thick lenses, the world to him is data rich, maybe too rich. He captures information, labels and files it, then retreats to his quieter land of internal musings. We communicate best by a kind of Braille. No words, no worries.

We married at home, a very small ceremony. James, Lisa, Maeva, and Margaux supported the four corners of the *chuppah*, the embroidered canopy beneath which we made our vows. There were tears. One drop landed on our *kettubah*, the marriage contract on fine parchment I decorated with intertwining patterns of leaves and flowers. There was joy. Cathy photographed the ceremony and the celebration down by the creek, and when we returned from our New Zealand honeymoon, she gave us a beautiful photo book of our wedding.

Today I keep our *kettubah* scroll loose, unframed in a cabinet in the great room, near the painted box that holds my mother's roses. Every few months I circle back and feel again the sense of loss and the sense of belonging captured by these accessible mementos. This is tangible contrast. This is how we learn. This is life.

Just last night I had a dream. As I woke the details faded away, but I was left with the essence. Ever since we married I have not felt like running away . . . not once.

Is it possible to be simultaneously safe and free, fully present as a woman and a soul, while being loved by another? After all, I see now loving is not safe. Not in the overarching, rainbow dream of safe, where the whole sky is decorated with proof of love.

Is anyone free? No, not in the boundless, joyous, trampoline of horizontal and vertical freedom we sometimes think we crave.

But at last I think I am safe enough, and free enough, to let myself be loved.

AFTER THE FIRE: RENEWAL

A year and a half after the firestorm in Sonoma County, Claudia and Erick moved to a cottage beside a creek about twelve miles away. There they planted vibrant gardens, and Erick built and decorated furniture to suit each room. Their new place is a 100-acre wonderland. Volcanic rock and sparse trees lend an Icelandic feel to the terrain, and their long-term arrangement with the owner is secure.

On our road, the seven burned-out lots of our neighbors have slowly transformed. Though trees are still missing, the new buildings are almost complete, some redesigned and some replicas of the past.

As the community renewal proceeds, my own "rebuild" continues as well. Melting my armor and learning to trust, connecting authentically with people—this all sounds good, but I have learned this requires more than the *idea* of change.

During the Jewish New Year this past autumn, at the two-year mark after the fire, I realized my son James was right. I must forgive myself for fleeing without warning others. During the ten days of awe, I meditated on letting go. It is time to begin anew.

In the Twill House, I set up my writing desk, brew some French press coffee, and ponder the past two years. The devastating fire scorched a hole in my nature girl story, yes. But even more important, the fire and its aftermath sparked a change that opened an entire new world.

I am not a murderer, and I mean no harm. The crushed man, my stillborn baby, Harry's death, and abandoning our neighbors during the firestorm, these I must forgive.

I recall my beginning on this planet, under the big blue bowl of sky, when I felt loved. Worthy. Known. Years of self-reliance, shielding myself from others, these are side effects of losing trust so long ago. Okay, then. What is so precious about *this*—what I have known, what I have done? I am ready to lower my guard and step into the unknown, into *something better*. Trust, the magic elixir that will dissolve my armor, waits for me there.

Acknowledgments and Gratitude

To all my family who read or heard countless versions, thank you for being so gentle with feedback. To my cousin Debby, whose constancy has been true through all our lives, I salute you. Thank you to my writing group, Linda Castrone, Millicent Susens, Melanie Vuyonovich, and Julie Dearborn, for patience, fun and useful insights. To Noelle Oxenhandler and Gillian Conoley, professors at Sonoma State, for inspiration and guidance. I am deeply grateful to Brooke Warner, publisher and founder at She Writes Press, for blazing the trail so many women now travel—thank you Brooke! To my sister authors at She Writes Press, Isidra Mencos, Lindsey Salatka, Catherine Drake, and Susan Speranza, thank you for your tenacious support throughout this past year. To wonderful editors Joanna Mitchell, Linda Castrone, and Jennifer Gray, you smoothed out the rough spots and kept me on course. And always, thank you to Chuck, my true companion, a mensch and mentor. I am blessed beyond my fondest dreams.

About the Author

Elisa Stancil Levine was born in Northern California and grew up beside the American River, the site of the California gold rush. She left high school at sixteen and as a young mother earned an AA degree, remodeled sixteen houses, and wrote for *Sacramento Magazine*. Her successful decorative art company, Stancil Studios, has won numerous awards and is now owned by her son, James. Elisa and her husband spend hours immersed in nature on Sonoma Mountain, hiking, horseback riding, and running in the forest. *This or Something Better* is her second book.

SELECTED TITLES FROM SHE WRITES PRESS

She Writes Press is an independent publishing company
founded to serve women writers everywhere.
Visit us at www.shewritespress.com.

Fire Season: A Memoir by Hollye Dexter. $16.95, 978-1-63152-974-0.
After she loses everything in a fire, Hollye Dexter's life spirals downward and she begins to unravel—but when she finds herself at the brink of losing her husband, she is forced to dig within herself for the strength to keep her family together.

There Was a Fire Here: A Memoir by Risa Nye. $16.95, 978-1-63152-045-7. After a devastating firestorm destroys Risa Nye's Oakland, California home and neighborhood, she has to dig deep to discover her inner strength and resilience.

Secrets in Big Sky Country: A Memoir by Mandy Smith. $16.95, 978-1-63152-814-9. A bold and unvarnished memoir about the shattering consequences of familial sexual abuse—and the strength it takes to overcome them.

Fourteen: A Daughter's Memoir of Adventure, Sailing, and Survival by Leslie Johansen Nack. $16.95, 978-1-63152-941-2. A coming-of-age adventure story about a young girl who comes into her own power, fights back against abuse, becomes an accomplished sailor, and falls in love with the ocean and the natural world.

Seasons Among the Vines: Life Lessons from the California Wine Country and Paris by Paula Moulton. $16.95, 978-1-938314-16-2. New advice on wine making, tasting, and food pairing—along with a spirited account of the author's experiences in Le Cordon Bleu's pilot wine program—make this second edition even better than the first.

Painting Life: My Creative Journey Through Trauma by Carol K. Walsh. $16.95, 978-1-63152-099-0. Carol Walsh was a psychotherapist working with traumatized clients when she encountered her own traumatic experience; this is the story of how she used creativity and artistic expression to heal, recreate her life, and ultimately thrive.